Praise for Out of the Question

"*Out of the Question* is a must read for any CEO seeking to elevate their leadership style. Incorporating more of the 'Learner's Mindset' in my daily work will be essential in leading our continued efforts of building high functioning teams capable of making the necessary adjustments in the dynamic healthcare marketplace."

Tom Carroll
CEO, South Shore Medical Center

"Milham and Parsons introduce the compelling 'Learner Mindset' that is a requirement for today's leaders. It's a game changer in leadership philosophy, and essential for unifying a workforce including the broad range of expectations from baby boomers to millennials. *Out of the Question* is a must read for executives pursuing continual improvement."

Mark Gilreath
Founder and CEO, Endochoice

"This concept is not a fad or some fly-by-night leadership theory . . . this transformative read will be applicable 100 years from now."

Robb Gomez
President, Paradigm Learning

"As leaders, we might have the answers, but it's the questions we need to get right. This book helps you engage more fully those around you in making the important decisions that drive your organization."

Verne Harnish
CEO, Gazelles
Author of Mastering the Rockefeller Habits *and* Scaling Up

"*Out of the Question* will help any leader take his or her results to the next level. The 'Learner Mindset' is the most important leadership skillset for the next decade."

David Hoffman
Director, Internet Security and Privacy Officer, Intel Corporation

"A compelling and relevant book for today's leaders committed to empowering their teams to greater and sustained results."

Ashish Lahoti
SVP, Wells Fargo Bank

"Coaching is a critical skill for any transformational leader. And, asking good questions—better considered, better formulated, better delivered—is a critical skill for any leader. Authors Parsons and Milham not only lay out a convincing argument for the foundational place of asking good questions, they give us a practical guide which any leader can use to become a better questioner and coach. This book helped me already."

John Shook
Chairman and CEO, Lean Enterprise Institute

"*Out of the Question* delivers a leadership blueprint to successfully lead today's workforce and provoke leaders to step into the required mindset to win!"

Ken Simonelic
Vice President of Information Technology, Televerde, Inc.

"The world is moving from old-fashioned bosses who know it all and tell subordinates what to do to a new type of leader who leads a team to discover both the problem and the most promising answer for testing. The problem for old-fashioned bosses—and I certainly have been one—is how to make the transition. What's needed is a wise coach. This book is that wise coach for any leader willing to learn."

Jim Womack
Founder and Senior Advisor, Lean Enterprise Institute

OUT of the QUESTION

QUESTION

HOW *CURIOUS* LEADERS *WIN*

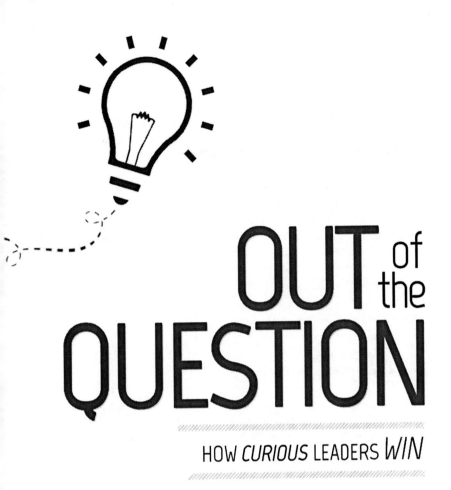

OUT of the QUESTION

HOW *CURIOUS* LEADERS *WIN*

GUY PARSONS / ALLAN MILHAM

Advantage®

Published by Advantage, Charleston, South Carolina.
Member of Advantage Media Group.

ADVANTAGE is a registered trademark and the Advantage colophon is a trademark of Advantage Media Group, Inc.

Printed in the United States of America.

ISBN: 978-159932-460-9
LCCN: 2014950316

Book design by George Stevens.

This publication is designed to provide accurate and authoritative information in regard to the subject matter covered. It is sold with the understanding that the publisher is not engaged in rendering legal, accounting, or other professional services. If legal advice or other expert assistance is required, the services of a competent professional person should be sought.

Advantage Media Group is proud to be a part of the Tree Neutral® program. Tree Neutral offsets the number of trees consumed in the production and printing of this book by taking proactive steps such as planting trees in direct proportion to the number of trees used to print books. To learn more about Tree Neutral, please visit **www.treeneutral.com**. To learn more about Advantage's commitment to being a responsible steward of the environment, please visit **www.advantagefamily.com/green**

Advantage Media Group is a publisher of business, self-improvement, and professional development books and online learning. We help entrepreneurs, business leaders, and professionals share their Stories, Passion, and Knowledge to help others Learn & Grow. Do you have a manuscript or book idea that you would like us to consider for publishing? Please visit **advantagefamily.com** or call **1.866.775.1696**.

FOREWORD

A llan Milham and Guy Parsons have created a fusion of two powerful thought processes found in altogether-too-few C-suite managers: Executive Coaching and Lean Thinking. As two experienced practitioners of both of these fine arts, the authors do more than just insist on a management methodology that hinges on asking questions, and, specifically, they ask that we ask the right kinds of questions.

Their prescriptions and suggestions come from long careers. Allan's expertise relates to his fully-articulated executive coaching style, which is highly personalized. Guy draws on his decades of experience as a thought leader, practitioner, and mentor to organizations and teams that want to emulate the success of archetypal lean organizations, such as Toyota and Danaher. Their skill sets have transformed enterprises, operating groups, and individuals in realms as diverse and vital to our economy as manufacturing, healthcare, finance, and professional services.

Both authors are pioneers in their fields. Allan's explanation of his own professional transformation is at the core of this book; and Guy's experience as one of the first lean leaders in the United States sets the scene for a very hands-on statement of mission, as well as a detailed, step-by-step path to successful implementation. The blending of their histories, with a clear prescription for curiosity, insight, and action, has already enriched my own personal and professional life, and I recommend this book to every person who aspires to lead and manage. The lessons to be learned from the authors' expertise span the full range of control of any organization: from line responsibility to the highest reaches of management and boards. As I often say, "Every activity in human experience is a process, and every process can be improved, continuously." Allan and Guy provide the reader with a roadmap and a methodology to optimize such efforts.

Unlike many of the self-proclaimed lean and coaching gurus I encounter in my own business environments, these two lucid commentators understand that this mentoring journey is based on principles, clarified by example, reinforced by curiosity, inspired by behaviors, and rooted in a sustainable culture of asking the right questions . . . and then listening very carefully to the answers. Readers should listen carefully to the play of words inherent in the phrase, "Out of the Question."

CLIFFORD F. RANSOM II

Founder and CEO, Ransom Research, Inc.,
"The Way of Lean Investing"

Life Member of the Shingo Prize for Operational Excellence

Past Chairman of the Board of Governors, The Shingo Institute

ACKNOWLEDGEMENTS

GUY

My 20 years of work in the continuous improvement community have been intensely collaborative. I have been fortunate to learn so much from so many that it is very difficult to single out specific contributions from specific individuals. My colleagues and partners, as well as my clients, have been invaluable sources of insight into how to foster the growth of people and the growth of organizations.

A few key people and organizations deserve special mention. Jim Womack and John Shook: friends, mentors and partners in thought for the past 20 years. Tom Foco: My close friend and long-term business partner. And to Peter Ickes and Brad Power, who are two intellectual powerhouses who keep me constantly on my game by asking all the right questions.

The Lean Transformation Group, my coauthors on the *Mapping to See* book and training package published at the Lean Enterprise Institute.

Dr. Henry Ting at the Mayo Clinic, who was my first partner in learning and adapting the Lean principles to complex healthcare issues.

To Verne Harnish of Gazelles Inc., who is the one person who really pushed and inspired me to put my many thoughts to paper.

To my 120-plus clients who have been my learning partners and have been so generous in so many ways.

To my wife, Carolyn Howard, for her insightful editorial and content contributions, and my children Guy and Elena, with whom I have practiced, and often fumbled, new ideas for working with people and teams. Thanks for your patience!

And, finally, to my co-author Allan, with whom I experienced the rich world of coaching firsthand as a client. I incorporated key coaching concepts in my work life, producing more income, less stress, and better client outcomes. Who better to partner with on the topic of leadership, given our combined perspectives?

ALLAN

The topic of leadership has been a complex and intriguing topic for decades, and I have appreciated observing the transformation many make from sole contributor, to manager, and then to leader. I define leadership as something that can be "always on" and is holistic in nature: in how we lead at work, at home, and in our communities. Those who emerge as leaders in our world have access to a full leadership spectrum, which is what this book is all about.

As I reflect on those who have left an imprint on me as I have studied, defined, and crafted my own signature leadership style, I want to acknowledge my early mentor Dr. Wen Chao Chen for serving as a genuine and authentic leader in a time when transparency was not in fashion.

To those who served in a leadership role during my days in corporate America: Gabe, Rich, Martha, Bob, Jeni, Brad, Anthony, and Marie.

To Karen and Henry House and Laura Whitworth, the founders of CTI (The Coaches Training Institute), for designing the Co-Active Leadership Program, which serves as one of the most profound leadership training programs globally, and helped shape who I am today.

To my leadership tribe: Carol, David, Elena, Gary, Jennifer, Marci, Phil, Rita, Steve, and Trudy, who, for fifteen years, have held a mirror up for me to claim the leader I am.

To my clients, who have invited me into their world to partner with them as they define, calibrate, and own their signature leadership style.

To my wife, Janis, who serves as an inspiration with her unique leadership style, which models transparency, authenticity, and curiosity, both in her role at work and at home as a wife and mother.

Finally, to my co-author, Guy, who lives in the power of the question with his insatiable appetite to lead continuous improvement initiatives with rigor, passion, and fun.

Table of Contents

Introduction

Tony Bartleson had enjoyed a solid career for two decades when his world got rocked. He had worked at Giltey Electrical since college and had learned the ropes from a no-nonsense boss. This boss held his cards close to his chest, and his temper flared when he sensed incompetence. Tony learned early on to go to his boss for answers and to follow faithfully his direction.

Tony adapted well and got results. Following his mentors led him to regular promotions. The company even invested in him, and he earned an Executive MBA on his tenth anniversary with the company. While Tony's self-esteem was never high, the promotions and advanced degree confirmed for him that he had a rightful seat in the boss's chair. When Tony was put in charge of his own people, he assimilated the personality and management style that he had observed in his boss.

In his twelfth year with the company, the business was impacted by a national recession, and Tony began to internalize the poor results. His self-doubt escalated, and he demanded more of his employees, giving ever-escalating, rapid-fire orders, and often assigning blame. Tony's style as an operator was to move fast and not to think too much about the future. He focused on whatever required attention at the moment. Those who wanted a career under Tony knew they had to operate fast or seek work elsewhere.

Tony's world changed when the board hired a new president with a leadership style quite different from Tony's. It became clear quickly that Tony's 20-year career at Giltey would come to a halt unless he made some changes.

The new president was an open and confident leader with a strong sense of curiosity. Among the changes he instituted was a 360-degree review process for the senior team. For the first time Tony discovered what employees really thought about him. He always said that he lived by an open-door policy, but he learned that few would walk through it for fear of running straight into his intimidating, know-it-all management style. To compound matters, Tony also saw that his new boss wasn't interested in having a team composed of anyone who had that kind of heavy-handed approach to leadership.

The new president had worked with Allan Milham in his previous job, and, because he was impressed by Tony's ability to get results (but not with the way he got them), the boss suggested that Tony speak with Allan to discuss how Tony might recalibrate his leadership style. Tony was open to the opportunity, and, with Allan as his coach, he began to look at how he could still get strong results in a way that empowered his team.

Allan began by introducing some new skills to Tony, such as doing a lot less telling and a lot more listening and inquiring; learning how to approach problems with a sense of curiosity, seeking first to understand and then be understood; and cultivating the ability to "pause and reflect" before he jumped to action. People were stunned by how these new skills affected Tony's behavior. In fact, one employee said to him, "I just need to check in with you. Did you get some life-threatening news? Are you okay?"

Slowly, Tony began to make the kind of fundamental shift we're calling for in this book: moving from a Knower to a Learner mindset. He also began to see how this shift could work for him, because when he started asking employees for their ideas, not only did they feel empowered and excited, they were also more innovative. His coworkers were willing to take more risks and bring more creative imagination to solving problems than before. Employees generated powerful new ideas and implemented changes that delivered significant impact on the company's bottom line.

The changes in Tony amazed many people around him. People started referring to him affectionately as the Old Tony and the New Tony. When he was doing well, they'd say, "Hey, New Tony, that is impressive." If he slipped into past behaviors, they'd say, "Hey, wait a minute. Is that Old Tony or New Tony talking?" Not only did his performance reviews and 360s improve markedly, he also got better results with a lighter, more inclusive style. Thanks to his new leadership approach, he had a lot more energy at the end of the day. His transformation was a huge success for the company, for its customers and employees, and for Tony's own well-being.

THE CASE FOR CHANGE

The business world changes continuously, and business leaders often need makeovers to maintain the pace. In the past, leaders arrived at work with an attitude of "I know," or "I have the answers and that's why I'm the boss," much as Tony did early in his career.

Today's leaders need a different mindset. In this book we will introduce a new leadership spectrum, with *Knower* leaders on one side, and *Learner* leaders on the other. We will then show you how to make a shift toward the Learner side of the spectrum in order to generate enhanced success as a leader.

People can no longer lead only from what they know and have experienced. The world is moving too fast, and there's too much to know to rely on one person's knowledge. We all need the collective creativity and knowledge of the team to move forward. Besides, the millennials who are now filling the workplace don't respond as well to a traditional command-and-control environment. Instead, leaders *and* their teams can benefit from adopting an attitude of curiosity and exploration. Both can learn how to ask big, open questions. When leaders operate from a Learner mentality, they benefit in a multitude of ways: employees feel respected and heard, which causes them to be more engaged, and a new environment laced with the power of possibility is created, from which new and better business solutions for customers arise. When leaders make the shift from a Knower to a Learner mentality, everyone wins, and the company's bottom line reflects that transformation.

WHY BE A LEARNER, NOT A KNOWER?

The topic of leadership has been around for a very long time; effective management affects all businesses, regardless of size or industry. All companies have needs, and people are recruited to fill those needs. Some of those people perform well, and, as a result, they move up through the different levels of management. All of a sudden, that contributor to the company becomes a leader. The shift comes with a lot of "atta boys" or "atta girls," a title, and a raise, but rarely with any personal leadership development. Few leaders pause to look at the shift that needs to be accomplished to go from a sole contributor mindset to a leader mindset.

Our work comes into play at precisely that transition point. We have 40 years of combined experience helping business leaders and teams attain enhanced outcomes: Allan, in the world of individual performance improvement, and Guy predominantly with teams on developing process excellence. When we transform leaders into Learners, rather than Knowers (and we'll dive deeper into this distinction in Chapter 1), a desire to engage ripples throughout the organization. More and more people want to join that organization. Culture becomes a magnet. We believe that human beings want to do good and want to do well. They want to be compensated for their work, but they also want to be inspired. Leaders have to accept as an article of faith that employees want to grow and learn. Unfortunately, too many organizations crush those simple desires.

One of the reasons this book is timely and relevant is the reality that people have more choices today than ever for how and where they work, especially as they become more entrepreneurial. Because people have choices, it's more important than ever that leaders get it right. When leaders foster growth and development, people want to stick around. Employees enjoy cultures where people are asked to participate, particularly when that participation serves the customers, the employees, shareholders, and the bottom line simultaneously.

This book fuses our separate skill sets and expertise—the personal side, which is the core of Allan's work, and the team side, which is the heart of Guy's consulting practice. We believe the conditions today are nearly perfect for this fusion of approaches. Leaders must move toward the behaviors and operating principles in this book if they want to succeed in our changing world. In the coming pages, we will show you how to identify for yourself and your team the differences between Knower and Learner behaviors. From there, we offer you a roadmap for leading from a place of greater curiosity in order to enhance team engagement, elevate your organization's culture, and attract, develop, and retain top talent.

CHAPTER 1

Leadership 101: Knowing versus Learning

complete spectrum of possibilities exists for leaders who operate within the Knower-Learner framework. At one end of the spectrum, on the left side, rests the Knower, the hard-nosed autocrat who thinks he knows where to go and likes to tell everyone exactly what to do to get there. Knowers derive authority from the answers they have, or form, in their heads. On the other end of the spectrum, the right side, are the Learners, who operate with openness and creativity. The Learner derives authority from fostering effective collaboration. Depending on our frame of reference, mood, the health of our ego, and the situation at hand, we all fall into different places on that spectrum. As Tony did in the opening story, we may also drift from one end of the spectrum to the other.

In this chapter, we'll go into additional detail about the differences between Knowers and Learners. The distinction is really about a leadership mindset.

People are not permanently fixed on either extreme end of the spectrum—total Knowers or total Learners. Most of us exist somewhere in the middle. What we're suggesting is that you shift yourself toward the learning side of things in order to become the most effective leader. You must determine where you fall on the spectrum, and then ask yourself, "Where do I want to be on that spectrum to provide the greatest impact?" With that awareness, you can develop the skills you need to practice leadership in a new way.

THE KNOWER vs. THE LEARNER
(THE GENERAL)   (THE GUIDE)

Directs	Discovers
Micromanages	Guides
Gives step-by-step instructions	Has a framework for finding an ideal path
Tells	Asks
Dwells on history/facts	Dwells on possibilities
Justifies position	Searches for solutions
Needs to know the answer	Is comfortable with "I Don't Know"
Is an authoritarian manager	Is an inquiry-based leader
Closed to input	Values input
Manipulates	Orchestrates
Is Rigid	Is flexible and curious
Is insecure or egocentric	Has a healthy ego
Demands obedience	Demands ideas

A SHIFT IN MANAGEMENT PHILOSOPHY

The distinction between the Knower and the Learner parallels old versus new management thinking. The old management theories of the 1950s centered on employees showing up to work, punching in, doing what they needed to do to, and then leaving. Business has changed a lot in 60 years, but there are still people in positions of authority who feel that they have to be very directive in order to be effective. The very first distinction in the chart, which describes key differences between the two mindsets, is between the Knower's directive kind of energy and the Learner's impulse to discover and explore.

The Knower's strength comes from his title, his degree, and his tenure. We've all seen the various letters strung after the name on business cards, which serve as self-attached merit badges. These practices justify being in a position to tell other people what to do. This mindset is old school. Learners in the new mindset believe that, while they may have more experience in a specific area, their primary job is to help themselves and their team ascertain the best way to get from point A to point B.

Military operations historically have been entirely organized around the Knower management style. The general would issue orders from the back of the lines. Soldiers would execute them, and then they'd return to tell the general what happened so he could decide what to do next. Today's modern military has blown that up (pun intended), moving to a model whereby soldiers in the field are given guidelines based on principles and told to use their own intelligence to make the best choices they can on the spot. Situations simply move too fast on the modern battlefield, just as they do in business, to do it any other way.

Today, many employees are aching to be a part of the solution process rather than being told what to do, but there are still a lot of old-school managers who feel they need to control what everybody does every day. Compare that to organizations which thrive as their leadership approaches things in a new way. Google, for example, currently has teams in which 14 percent of the members don't have a college education. Despite the fact that Knowers like to wear their degrees like merit badges, Google's research has shown that GPA and test scores don't predict anything. Instead, Google looks for candidates who can demonstrate humility and ownership, who know when to lean in and when to step back. Adam Bryant, Google's senior vice president of People Operations, has said, "The least important attribute we look for is expertise. Instead, we look for somebody who has high cognitive ability, is innately curious, is willing to learn, and has emergent leadership skills."

Google so believes in the importance of learning that the company tells its people to spend 20 percent of their paid time working on projects of interest. Google management doesn't even ask people to spend that time on known products. They are confident that people, when given space to be creative, will come up with new and interesting ideas. Google gives employees the opportunity to explore with a simple guardrail: Follow your instincts and be serious. That's an example of the Learner mindset at its best, and how leadership can instill that mindset in employees.

So what's behind a policy like that? What does Google hope will happen? We know that Learner environments foster possibility thinking. Most important, possibility thinking fosters the magic of wonder. Instead of being enslaved by a head-down mentality, wherein you plow through your work and put out the next fire, you pause and imagine what it would be like if one of your ideas turned into the next billion-dollar product. Google lets people create products inside Google Labs. Eight out of ten of those projects run briefly and then get shut down, but two out of ten become big winners like Google Maps or Google Drive. Google rests at the other edge by promoting creative behavior ahead of business purpose.

> Ask yourself what it would be
> like to take a couple of 10-minute
> breaks during the day to walk
> and wonder.

Google and the military are two completely different examples of this new way of thinking, but both illustrate the idea that the world is moving toward more respect for a sense of curiosity and for leading without the constraint of first knowing the answers. Old mindset leaders were expected to know exactly where they were trying to go and prescribe for their teams how to get there step by step. Today you can lead without even knowing the exact destination or end point.

Classic business strategy attempts to use a competitive framework to map out product and sales initiatives in advance of taking action, but there is another, equally valid school of thought, well explained by author David Hurst and others, which insists that strategy emerges from the actions as they unfold in a business. As the German general Von Moltke put it long ago, "No plan survives first contact with the enemy." Learner leaders will continuously absorb what's happening around them and adjust, rather than having a mighty plan that's been formed by only a few "smart people" at a strategy session once a year (see David Hurst, *Business Mastery in a Chaotic World*, 2012).

The difference between the Knower approach and the Learner approach is the difference between a planned trip and a journey of discovery. A generation back, AAA, the travel association, would give you what it called a TripTik, which got you from point A to point B as quickly as possible, even though you might miss out on a bunch of amazing things just a couple of miles off to your left or right. It's a different mentality when you put the right things in your backpack and the right ideas in your head and set off on a journey, not knowing exactly where you'll end up or how you'll get there. (The journey, of course, needs some basic guidelines such as a clear purpose, budget, timeline, etc.) You just know that it's going to be an interesting learning opportunity, so you keep your mind open and curious.

THE POSITIVE ASPECT OF PROBLEMS

There is a famous story about a senior executive in Japan who traveled to one of his company's plants and asked the plant manager, "How are things going?" The plant manager replied, "No problem." The visiting executive then said, "No problem is a problem. Either you can't see your problems, in which case we need a new manager, or there are no problems, in which case we need no manager." The moral of the story is that problems are good. The leader's job is to be continuously curious about how things are working and to constantly work with the team to make them better.

PROBLEMS ARE GOOD   NO PROBLEMS ARE BAD

THE BENEFITS OF LEARNER-BASED THINKING

The primary reason to consider change in your leadership mindset is this: People are hungry for it, and the millennials demand it. Such attitudes are becoming less of an option and more of a requirement for companies if they want to be successful. Employees, especially good employees, won't stick around for anything less than a Learners' environment.

Many additional benefits motivate Learner managers. Consider the following if you're wondering whether making this kind of change is worth your time and effort:

BETTER OUTCOMES

If we were to be extreme for a moment and imagine that you, as a leader, are a 100 percent Knower and completely directive, then you can only go as far as your own imagination can take you. On the other hand, if you are a Learner capable of engaging the minds of people around you by asking good, genuine questions, then you have the opportunity to go where the collective imagination of every person on your team can take you. You draw from a deeper well when solving problems or coming up with new ideas. As a result, the probability of success rises significantly.

MORE ENGAGEMENT AND INVESTMENT

Getting people involved doesn't just result in a greater possibility for positive outcomes; it also creates more motivated employees, employees ready to invest in those outcomes. When you lead and ask questions from a mindset of genuine curiosity and you encourage your people to contribute their own best answers to get to an end point, your coworkers become joint owners in the process. The team owns the journey, as opposed to the leader owning the journey and everyone else functioning as mindless soldiers. In the corporate world, we call that engagement. When people are drawn in and engaged in the process, they care more about seeing it through—and that investment of caring offers huge results.

FASTER LEARNING

Learner leaders who know how to let go of the reigns of control and the need to have all the answers can really increase the rate of the company learning. When people are allowed to think openly, experiment, and even fail without recrimination, Learners comprehend that these are positive effects. A philosophy called "fail forward fast," means you learn so much from failure that it's better to get started and make mistakes than it is to hold back and get everything perfect before launching your product. If you create a dialogue with your customers and they tell you, "The product should do this, not that," then your business can evolve more quickly. If leaders can let go of their need to be right and embrace the benefits of failing forward fast, they're going to win.

REDUCED PRESSURE ON THE LEADER

In today's complex and changing world, it's simply impossible for one person to know all the answers. When leaders shift from an "I have to know" mindset to recognizing it's acceptable to say, "I don't know, but let's figure it out," their job gets simplified. With an orientation of "we," the shared responsibility draws on shared knowledge and intellect, which is much more expansive than a "me" orientation. This process of leading can really reduce the amount of stress leaders have to shoulder. They no longer have to know everything themselves or control situations. They get to lead in a humane way by saying, "We're all in this together."

REDUCED RISK

In a Knower environment, mistakes get covered up and unusual or unexpected results are often hidden. A *blame-and-hide* culture is risky when people hide problems, issues don't get resolved, and crucial learning and improvement don't take place. In a Learner environment, inquiry is celebrated and everyone is encouraged to find and pull loose threads, which enhances the likelihood that you'll discover the root cause of problems. And by engaging the team as active participants, the door to communication stays open, which allows for greater contribution and greater freedom of expression, which in turn minimizes risks.

ALLAN ON WHAT KILLS CREATIVE THINKING

Imagine a manager who came into the advertising department and said, "We are missing our budget badly. We have to come up with a home run. You've got two hours to figure this out. Go."

That is probably not the best way to access innovation and creativity, as we are now learning from modern neuroscience. Scientists are rewriting the book on how the brain processes information. People are forced into pressure-cooker situations, and then leaders wonder why positive results are not forthcoming. The easier model to emphasize, allows the Learner to lead through a sense of curiosity and openness with questions that get everyone involved, invested, and drawing on their common experience and knowledge. Imagine what would happen if people weren't always under that pressure to succeed. How might innovation and creative thinking benefit?

GUY ON THE CHANGING ATTITUDES OF YOUNGER WORKERS

I have a 16-year-old son who worked at a restaurant. He was successful, and well liked by the customers, but he quit after six weeks because he said the owner of the restaurant didn't want to discuss different ways of getting the job done. He said, "Dad, I don't want to work in a place like that." Now, that might have reflected a little bit of his father's influence, but the point is that younger people today want to be involved in how decisions are made. They don't want to just be told what to do. They don't want to hear, "I hired you for your hands.

Leave your head at the door," which is a famous quote from Henry Ford. That model doesn't work anymore.

Let's face it, if you want to show respect, you don't do it by ordering people around. At its core, this up-and-coming generation wants to be respected. They can no longer rely on lifetime job security and pensions, so you have to show them respect to get their inspired day-to-day efforts. Otherwise, just like my son, even if they're successful at their job, they may look for the door.

WHAT MAKES AN EFFECTIVE LEARNER LEADER?

Now that you have a better idea of why Learner leaders have a distinct advantage in today's business world, the question is: How do you move yourself closer to that end of the spectrum? The qualities you will need to cultivate include curiosity, open-spiritedness, and humility. You must be willing to say, "There are a lot of things I don't know."

> Ponder, when you're asked about something you don't know, how readily you will admit you don't know, rather than feeling obliged to produce some sort of answer.

As you migrate toward Learner leadership, you start to realize that the more you explore and learn about something, the more you understand what you don't know. The unknown keeps getting bigger in front of you, not the other way around. On life's journey, many move from being a student to becoming a master. Allan would add that in the Learner mindset, the student becomes the master, who becomes the student, who becomes the master, and so on. In other words, it's always revolving. The problem arises when the student becomes the master and then winds up closed to additional learning. In other words, over time, mastery is no longer masterful.

There's an element of ego in the idea that there's nothing more to learn. We all come with ego, but it's the insecure ego of Knowers that makes them need to know and control. They move into a position of authority and become fearful they won't succeed, which is why they need to always be in the know and in control. Those with a healthy ego don't have that fear, which allows them to be generous and humble. When you're insecure, you're always going to try to claim credit. When you're a Learner, you adopt the mindset that you're part of the team and you're all going somewhere together. That attitude leads to generosity about credit and ownership of the future. When you can be generous and have a strong sense of curiosity, the team naturally forms around getting the job done. When you're stingy and try to collect credit for yourself, the team won't respond as effectively. A healthy ego is what allows you to move from me to we. This shift permits things to happen in a team or organization that go far beyond what we experience today.

Learner leaders are secure enough to understand that, while they have authority, they don't have to be responsible for everything or to maintain direct control at all times. In the Learner mindset, if a team agrees that someone is responsible for getting something done, regardless of his title or role in the organization chart, then he's responsible and people will defer to him. Delegation of responsibility is a high-performance way to get things accomplished.

An example of this can be found at Toyota, where the Sochi, the chief engineer for a new vehicle, such as the Prius, has no direct authority and few staff members. The Sochi, however, is responsible for bringing a whole new automotive platform into existence. When he comes into your office, you know who he is and why he's coming to see you, and you participate. You don't do it because he's going to fill out your performance review next week. You do it because you want to help make things happen.

We've all met people who, within just a few minutes, have told us something about what they own, the length of their title, or where they went to school. People who brag about such things are typically not Learners. Think about what you usually ask people when you meet them for the first time at a cocktail party. In America, we tend to ask, "What do you do?" In Europe, historically, that question almost never comes up (though this may be changing). Instead, people say, "Tell me about your family," or "Where do you come from?" The conversation starts on who you are rather than what you do, and the questioner is more likely to be genuinely curious about the answer. Consciousness of these distinctions in approach will help you move your set point on the Knower-Learner spectrum.

Being a Learner leader means leading from a mindset of genuine, humble curiosity. When you come from that vantage point, you enhance your chance to ensure great results through others and to reach your highest potential. At its core, a learning culture is about opening instead of closing doors to the future. You want to open and leave open as many doors as possible as you charge forward.

KNOWER-LEARNER QUIZ

To learn where you fall on the knower-learner spectrum, answer the following questions:

1. How often do team members come to you for answers when they don't know what to do?

    Most of the time   *Sometimes*   *Rarely*

    _____

2. In the course of a typical day, how often do you talk rather than listen in your conversations with others?

    Most of the time   *Sometimes*   *Rarely*

    _____

3. How often do you finish other people's sentences?

    Most of the time   *Sometimes*   *Rarely*

    _____

4. When someone is slower or not thinking at your level, how often do you lose patience?

    Most of the time   *Sometimes*   *Rarely*

    _____

5. If people come to you with a question, how likely are you to provide an answer rather than adopt a mood of curiosity?"

    Most of the time   *Sometimes*   *Rarely*

    _____

6. How often do you prepare for meetings by arriving with a solution and a strategy to persuade others toward your solution?

    Most of the time   *Sometimes*   *Rarely*

    _____

7. How often do you like being thought of as "really smart" versus being known as someone who makes people think?

    Most of the time   *Sometimes*   *Rarely*

    _____

8. How often are you in a "head-down / plow through" mindset versus intentionally fostering a mood of wonder and possibility thinking during your day?

    Most of the time   *Sometimes*   *Rarely*

    _____

9. How often do you put on a poker face that covers up your uncertainty in a difficult situation?

    Most of the time   *Sometimes*   *Rarely*

    _____

10. How often do you believe showing vulnerability at work should be avoided at all cost?

Most of the time   *Sometimes*   *Rarely*

READING YOUR RESULTS

If you had seven or more "Rarely" responses circled, you are naturally oriented to the Learner mindset. Conversely, if you had seven or more "Most of the time" responses circled, you are probably oriented towards the Knower mindset.

Everyone falls somewhere on the Knower-Learner spectrum, and there is no value assigned to your score. Rather, your quiz results offer an initial baseline of where you are on the spectrum right now. You can use this book and its proposed techniques and skills as a framework for shifting to a learner mindset. Our assertion is that in today's workplace, adopting the Learner mindset is the way to win, for you and your colleagues.

CHAPTER 2

Think Before You Speak: The Power of the Pause

lbert Einstein once said, "If I had 60 minutes to solve an important problem, I would spend 55 minutes on defining the problem and five minutes on the solution." When it's time to step up and lead, you can build the skills of self-awareness concerning your leadership style and mindset. When you know and understand the impact your leadership has on the situation and the people involved, your likelihood of success rises significantly.

Our proposal is simple: Before you engage, you should literally *pause* and indulge in some structured thinking. This methodology will allow you to set yourself up for a qualitatively different experience. Instead of jumping right in and acting on instinct, reflect and ask yourself:

⇨ Who am I in this circumstance?

⇨ What's my role?

⇨ What outcomes are we seeking?

⇨ Is there anything I need to do to prepare myself to engage in this conversation powerfully?

This self-questioning can be a lot harder than it sounds. We've worked with countless business leaders over the years who say they understand the importance of the pause, but, when we really drill down and examine how well they use it, they actually score very poorly. We stress that it's crucial that leaders get this step right because, without it, they'll always be leading from behind. All too often they aren't able to prepare themselves in the most effective way and they aren't able to orchestrate productive interactions among colleagues and team members.

One of the reasons leaders find this process so difficult is because they're dealing with today's perceived speed of business, with endless to-do lists and the moment-to-moment demands that are placed on people in organizations. So many of us get caught up in that adrenaline rush to go, go, go—do, do, do. When that happens, we walk into meetings with no plan for the desired outcome. Because of the pressure for speed, we enter into conversations without an inquiring mindset that allows for fresh and relevant outcomes.

Despite these pressures, you need to think about the context and the circumstances from the outset. You want to ask yourself where this particular situation needs to conclude. Starting with the end in mind gives you clarity. A little simple preparation allows you to construct the right questions and to adapt to the right attitude in order to encourage an exchange of new ideas, innovation, and creative thinking.

Failure to plan makes you prone to what we call "triggering situations." When people are triggered, they're in what we call a "nowhere mindset," and they can actually sabotage the environment with anger or other emotions. Instead of being ripe for "possibility thinking," the environment becomes one of blame, defensiveness, and finger pointing. Obviously, that system is not a winning model; we encourage you to stop and reflect before engaging in any meaningful engagement with colleagues, customers, suppliers, etc.

If you can take a moment to pause purposefully and formulate a plan before engaging in active questions (the process which we'll talk about in the next chapter), you augment your chances at being successful. This approach allows you to not only design a strategy to win, but also to recognize and reinforce the mindset you need have in order to foster that collaborative, one-plus-one-equals-three atmosphere.

> Ask yourself how often you take the time to pause and reflect as opposed to keeping your foot pinned to the gas pedal in your daily activity.

"A problem well stated is a problem half solved."

—*CHARLES KETTERING*

USING THE PAUSE

As you reflect on your leadership style, take an active moment to clear away the noise of all the other things that may be running around in your head and put some real, directed focus on the topic at hand. If you do not follow the procedure, you're unlikely to put creative energy into the process.

Obviously, in any given leader's day, mundane activity is often present with things that need to be dealt with and don't require any sort of active, careful management. On those occasions, you just do what needs to be done, but there are other times when something happens and you have to choose to either respond quickly, in a reactive way, or pause to reflect and manage the situation productively to reach the desired outcome.

Louis Pasteur, who invented pasteurization and the small pox vaccine, once said, "Chance favors the prepared mind." In order to be creative and invent something as powerful as pasteurization or vaccines, Pasteur needed an open, clear mind and a structured way of thinking.

> Ask yourself how often, when things don't go according to plan, you pause to reflect and learn before charging forward.

Once you learn how to pause, you can move from *reactive* to *active* management of an important situation. A spectrum still exists, but if you ponder where you stand, many circumstances will cause you, hopefully, to say, "Gee, this situation calls for something more than just immediate action. I need to reflect first before I engage with my audience."

For example, when your sales manager announces to you that the team is 30 percent short of its goals and that it's only two days until the end of the month, it would be easy for you to unleash an angry response. The opportunity, however, would be to pause and think about how you can engage productively in that moment. Many leaders would respond by firing back, "How could *you* let this happen?" Your role, however, could prompt you to ask, "How has our process allowed us to get this far into the month before discovering we're missing our targets?" Knowers will justify, looking to the past to explain why something external caused the poor results. Learners look to the future, curious about the possibilities for resolving the problem.

How might you respond if a rising star walks into your office and says, "You know what? I think I've had enough here and I'm quitting." A surprise announcement like that could make you angry because of all the time and energy you invested in this person's growth, but you have options here. You can pause and reflect before you speak and then ask a genuine question such as, "What circumstances have led you to this decision? Is there anything we could do to change your mind?" You have to avoid the automatic response and sidestep the trigger, in order to come at the problem from an inquiring mindset that lets you gain important feedback on why a "rising star" wants to leave. An initial pause will allow you to accomplish that all-important mission.

MINDFUL LEADERSHIP

A *pause* is the first step is to a productive conversation. In that pause, it's important to flush out all the distracting noise surrounding the circumstance. Many leaders are well known for having mastered this art. Jeff Bezos, who runs Amazon, is a perfect example. When an Amazon team is preparing to brainstorm or embrace a new topic, an executive usually says something such as, "Here's what I want you to read before the meeting." Bezos invites everyone into the room, hands out the reading material, and says, "Let's read this now. No e-mail, phone calls, or disturbances. Let's all sit and read for half an hour before we discuss this topic." That process gives everyone a chance to reflect in a focused way before any initiation of conversation, rather than storming into decisions. Bezos leads his team by example when he suggests, "Let's cut out the noise. Let's not be in our native environment. Instead, let's be in a quiet, secure place and think carefully before we make decisions."

Another well-regarded leader is Bill Gross, the founder of PIMCO, one of the largest fixed-income investment managers in the world. In a CNN interview he stated, "The most important part of my day isn't on the trading floor. Every day at 8:30 a.m., I get up from my desk and walk to a health club across the street. I do yoga and work out for probably an hour and a half . . . some of my best ideas literally come from standing on my head doing yoga. I'm away from the office, away from the noise, away from the Bloomberg screens, not to mention that standing on your head increases the blood flow to your brain. After about 45 minutes of riding the exercise bike and maybe 10 or 15 minutes of yoga, all of a sudden some significant light bulbs seem to turn on. I look at that hour and a half as a valuable time of the day."

Turning off the external noise is so important that Gross is willing to take time to do it in the middle of prime trading hours. His track record of success attests to the value of such discipline. We could cite many examples, including Arianna Huffington of the *Huffington Post*; the founder of Bridgewater Associates, Ray Dalio; executive chairman of Ford Motor Company, Bill Ford; and Oprah, who all say that things which encourage this kind of reflection, such as meditation or yoga, are key to their ability to be successful.

> Ask yourself how many minutes a day you stop everything, unplug, and drop into a quiet state of mindfulness.

While some use meditation or yoga to help reflect, others find it useful to structure the day so that they're ready to engage in difficult stuff. Author Stephen King, for example, writes "2,000 adverbless" words a day, while Tom Wolf has a strict quota of 1,800 words per day. Many well-known artists commit to highly structured days so that during the times when they want to be creative, they have clear minds and can let their creativity flow. Such discipline requires active management of their day to ensure that creative moment.

Each of us must find our best path. We often ask clients, "What kind of daily practice would help you stay grounded throughout the day for greatest impact?" We want leaders to look for ways to unplug and give the mind the rest it needs to flourish. And the more you, as a leader, practice this kind of reflection, the more you will be able to call upon internal inquiry when challenging circumstances arise. Practice and discipline are essential, but once you master the technique, pausing will give you the opportunity to form a point of view and actively manage your circumstance rather than reacting in the moment.

DEFINING DESIRED OUTCOMES

In his business, Allan will ask, "For the sake of what? What's the desired outcome?" In a meeting or a presentation, he'll ask, "What outcome would delight you?" His question permits leaders to articulate questions that will guide them toward the desired outcomes. (More on forming these questions in the next chapter.)

WHAT DOES IT MEAN TO REFLECT AS A LEADER?

We often see leaders "act first, reflect later." It's a syndrome of "Ready, Fire, Aim." We challenge people to reshuffle that sequence so that actions become intentional, in order to accomplish big, positive impacts.

In his coaching, Allan uses an analogy in which he asks clients to imagine they have been invited to meet the President of the United States. What would you do? You would most likely clear the decks and get yourself as grounded and prepared as possible in the face of such a big event and a big opportunity. In the time you took to prepare, you'd almost surely ask yourself, "What would be a great outcome? What would be something that would stick with me forever? What kinds of things should I ask or talk to him about to get that desired outcome?" If you have not done that advance work, you could squander the opportunity with just a handshake and regret your missed opportunity.

What Allan proposes is that clients strive to go into their meetings with extraordinarily focused attention. Think about how much attention you're giving to focus on one or two topics and do not squander the moment.

The pause enables the power of our intuition to come to the forefront. Those seeds of intuition, those possibilities, those glimmers of something new, come into our brain almost in the form of a whisper. If you're running hard, if you're externally focused, you can miss those whispers and the whole intuitive process can falter.

The need for help in this area just seems to grow and grow. Indeed, the field of professional leadership coaching exists precisely to fill this gap. Leaders spend significant dollars on coaching annually to have someone help them look in the mirror and reflect on their behavior and how they're performing.

Neuroscientific studies of the last 10 years have turned our thinking on its head, if you will pardon the pun. Your purposeful or thinking brain, which is called the prefrontal cortex, is separate from something called the amygdala. The amygdala, sometimes called our lizard brain, is the part of our anatomy that is wired for "fight or flight." The amygdala is what fires off adrenaline, which is helpful if you need to escape a burning building. In most situations today, however, if that system gets triggered, then you've lost control and it's much harder to manage the situation for an ideal outcome.

Reflection or mindfulness are tools to keep your thoughts and actions running through the active part of your brain before it gets to the reactive part of your brain. You benefit because you don't send that absolutely destructive e-mail or say something you'll regret. How many stories have we all heard of people who, at the height of the moment, banged out an e-mail "scud missile," only to pay the price for it later?

George Kohlrieser, author of *Hostage at the Table*, and a world-renowned hostage negotiator, discusses brain science in terms of how negotiators have to manage circumstances carefully to gain successful outcomes. In order to make progress with the hostage taker, the negotiator must build a relationship, however unnatural, in order to move the hostage taker from a highly stressed and reactive mode to one of thought and reason. Hours may be spent talking about family and life history to move the hostage taker away from a fight-or-flight mode and into a position where reason can be introduced. When we understand precisely how our brains work, we do not have to rely on knee-jerk responses; we can prepare ourselves to hunt for creative solutions and genuinely novel thinking.

Of course, not every situation is as critical as a hostage negotiation, but the same idea applies, adjusted for scale. If you address a relatively minor issue, you may need to pause only for a half a minute before opening your mouth. On the other hand, if you are served with legal papers that might put you in jail, you're obviously going to need to spend a lot more time thinking before you respond. We call this learned reaction, "rightsizing the response."

Most people don't put the right kind of time and effort into the right kind of problem. They just toss out the quickest response that they can. We've both attended many meetings where people throw solutions at problems as if they were Western gunslingers. They seem to think the first one with an answer wins. They're not pausing and really absorbing the circumstances or socializing ideas with others. This "pause and reflect" approach is meant to be an antidote to leaders slinging solutions at problems, slapping them on the table, and saying, "Do this!" Instead, we want them to say, "Tell me what you think the best three possible solutions are and let's discuss their strengths and weaknesses."

We're not suggesting everybody should become a Zen master, but there are a lot of things people can do to prepare their minds. Some people work out before big meetings. A lot of brain research suggests getting a good night's sleep before you engage is extraordinarily valuable. Another kind of preparation is to learn to say, "Can we address this tomorrow?" Frankly, no matter how well you prepare yourself, some days you're not going to be in the right frame of mind to handle a situation at the moment it arises.

The pause is partly personal and partly situational. The benefit is that you can, under most circumstances, take a moment to assess, think, and manage actively. This process expands the potential for positive outcomes and significantly reduces risk. Risk comes when you charge forward without planning.

GUY ON HOW HIS LIZARD BRAIN LET HIM DOWN

I personally lost a $90,000 contract by letting my lizard brain take charge. A client asked me to hold a significant block of time for his use. About three weeks into the quarter, he sent me a note that read, "Oh, by the way, we've decided to move that work into the next quarter." I can't fill my consulting days in a matter of minutes, so the client had, basically, wasted a block of my time, and I'd never be able to get the revenue back.

I wrote back asking when this decision had been made. The answer made it clear that the client had made the decision a month or more previously, but he hadn't bothered to share that fact with me. So I immediately sent back an e-mail that read, "This move on your part does not reflect the kind of respect and partnership that we're looking for in a business relationship. You have stolen my time and I can't get it back." The wording came from my lizard brain and was not my usual careful phraseology. The client was furious and canceled the contract. Now, when I sense my blood pressure rising, I often ask my business partner or wife to do a sanity check before I hit the send button in a heated exchange. You sometimes don't know if your amygdala has taken over and you're responding from emotion, or whether you're responding from careful planning. We all have to ask ourselves: How many things have gone south because we acted on a quick, lizard-brained response instead of a thoughtful, carefully planned response?

ALLAN ON TECHNIQUES TO CREATE THE PAUSE

Pause Button

Let us offer a technique that works well for leaders: Imagine you have an invisible remote control connected to your head that allows you to hit the pause button, providing you with time to think. Many leaders feel that everything has to happen in the here and now, and they feel compelled to respond to everything immediately. This condition does not have to prevail. If you give most people time to reflect and ponder, you will get a far better response than if you're standing there saying, "I've got to know now." Unfortunately, we've gotten into these fast-food, microwave, everything-in-a-nanosecond patterns, which has a seriously damaging impact on the quality of our work.

W.A.I.T.

Years ago, when Allan first began his study of the craft of coaching, he was introduced to the acronym, W.A.I.T., for "Why am I talking?" If you're extroverted and come alive when engaged with others, you're going to naturally want to talk things out.

W.A.I.T. reminds you that you don't have to feel compelled to fill the silence. Instead, you can ask, "Why am I talking?" You can make sure there's a real purpose to what you're saying before you open your mouth (if you open it at all).

Interruptions

Research shows that, for knowledge work, a single interruption can cause you to derail and lose 10 to 30 minutes of effort. Imagine how much time is wasted between e-mails, telephone calls, and open-door policies. Most of us live in an environment prone to constant interruption, so we are losing the battle. For a deeper dive into this topic read Dan Markovitz' book, *A Factory of One.*

> Ask yourself how you can gain control over interruptions. Do you silence your e-mail, use the do-not-disturb button on your phone, or telecommute when you need uninterrupted time?

How often are you escalating
the need for a response, making
it "urgent," when, in fact, it does
not need an immediate answer?

GUY ON DEDICATING QUIET TIME

I often ask clients to use their calendars to schedule themselves frequent
one-hour blocks away from the day to do thoughtful work. The idea is that
when you need to do creative, thoughtful work, you can't do it in thin slices
between other things. You need some quiet, desk-cleared opportunities to
do careful thinking. We've learned that when people get that kind of quality
time, their output doubles. Literally doubles. So plan for it in your calendar.

I worked with Starbucks on a holiday guide planning process that required
13 weeks to get a giant book prepared for the holidays. The company tried
an experiment in which it allocated a room without phones or e-mails, and
let people work in a kind of protected zone where they were only bothered
by family or really important interruptions. By setting up the dedicated
space, they were able to convert thirteen weeks of work into five weeks.
All that time was saved just by turning down the noise of multitasking and
interruptions.

Imagine how much more creative and effective they were. A dedicated space
shrank the amount of effort significantly and quality rose dramatically.

Do you use the do-not-disturb button on your cell phone?
How can you design non-negotiable white space on your

calendar for mindful reflection twice a day? Here are some suggestions:

⇨ Turn off the automatic notification feature in your e-mail. Do not succumb to the tyranny of getting distracted by that little flashing icon in the lower-right-hand side of your computer screen.

⇨ Use a spare conference room to create a distinct space that triggers focused effort. Dedicate yourself to this habit, and you will find that just entering the space triggers a habit of intense productivity.

⇨ Check your e-mail at fixed times each day and inform others of this habit so they will know when to expect a reply.

⇨ Consider noise-cancelling headphones. They work well, but most importantly, when you are seen using them, people will only interrupt you for really important matters.

Ask yourself how you can protect your environment and maximize the reflection time required for critical thinking.

PAUSE, REFLECT, RECALIBRATE

What happens when you look in the mirror and reflect? We believe that you will find that your brain becomes calm and thoughts become clear. You're able to increase the opportunities for creativity. You also reduce the chance of missteps, which can consume an awful lot of energy when you're trying to take back a poorly formed statement. When you can pause before speaking, you significantly increase your chances for a successful conversation.

In legal negotiations, the parties sometime agree to what is formally called "a cooling-off period." In the middle of negotiations, one party will say, "You know what? Let's pause and have a cooling-off period. We can come back to this topic tomorrow." Good negotiators realize that people often respond, not from their thoughtful minds, but from the emotional or fight-or-flight part of their brains. This process seldom produces good outcomes for either party.

> Ask yourself whether, when things escalate, you are able to call a time-out, rather than succumb to a fight-or-flight response.

Guy likes to use this line with leaders: "Control the controllables because everything else is going to happen." Recalibration is a great word to describe looking at a situation and identifying which aspects you should try to manage. Determine what can be known and what can't ever be known, then move on to the questions where you have a span of control. Again, the most important aspect of this skill is to understand clearly that, as a leader, you're managing actively—as opposed to responding reflexively—to the daily obstacles that come at you.

A recalibration occurs when people realize they can manage much more of their business day than they had assumed previously, beyond the hectic frenzy of e-mails, texts, phone calls, open-office policies, and overly filled calendars. Recalibration is evident when you can establish a practice of pausing, waiting, and asking yourself some careful questions about what's happening before you react. If you identify what you can control (and what you can't hope to control), you can be successful at recalibration. If you can make active choices about these things, if you can recognize that your biggest opportunity rests on the invention of a solution with your colleagues, and if you can avoid striving to have all the answers yourself, then you are recalibrating!

It's not just that you derive benefits from pausing. There's a price that is paid when one does not reflect and recalibrate. We've discussed the hectic pace of daily life today and the many pressures people face. Think about how many folks are coming home with their red light on from work, absolutely depleted because of the demands of today's workplace, and consider the ripple effect that this stress has on the rest of their lives. They have no energy for their spouse, partner, or children. This exhaustion is almost an epidemic, but recalibrating can have a significant impact on the way we live and lead our lives way beyond our work.

PAUSE AND CALIBRATE: FOUR GUIDELINES

1. Build in breaks for pauses throughout your day to provide time for regular reflection.

2. Reflect on your mood and the overall situation and ask what needs calibrating?

3. Ask authentic, genuine, and creative questions to ensure greater impact.

4. Lead with the Learner mindset, accessing the "observer's view," allowing yourself to monitor your impact throughout any engagement.

WHAT IS THE OBSERVER'S VIEW?

The observer's view is a technique of detaching yourself from the immediacy of what you're doing to look at the overall situation as if you were a third-party observer. Successful employment of this technique will enhance your effectiveness as a leader.

CHAPTER 3

Leading by Learning: What Is the Question?

B
y using questions, you can take a trip with others through uncharted territory, as opposed to being trapped alone on a prescribed route. We discussed in Chapter 1 the difference between a trip using the old-fashioned AAA TripTik, versus taking a real journey. The TripTik tells you exactly how to get from Kalamazoo to Boston with no deviations. A *journey* lets you participate in a learning adventure. You and colleagues get to use your collective intelligence to pick an enlightening path. Boston is still the destination, but the road to get there is not prescribed.

Whatever journey you undertake, you can go further, you can go faster, and you can do it more effectively by coming in with a Learner mindset. When you do, your horizons expand dramatically through the collective creative intelligence of your team.

QUESTIONING AS A TOOL

Many different frameworks for using questions have been discussed throughout history, as far back as the Socratic Method. For example, interrogation is a key technique in the legal field for examining witnesses.

Our purpose here is slightly different. We want you to think of questions as a starting point for taking a team on a journey. If leaders use just what's in their own head to take a team somewhere, they are capped by their own knowledge. On the other hand, if leaders ask genuine, open questions of the team—and that doesn't mean giving up responsibility for where the team needs to go—they are no longer limited to just what they know. Everyone can participate in getting to a new place.

The distinction we want to make here is between open thinking and closed thinking. When a question is asked as the result of open thinking, it is fundamentally rooted in curiosity. Of course, questions can be asked that are not motivated by curiosity. Lawyers, for example, tend to ask closed questions, as it's conventional wisdom in the legal world that you never ask a question for which you don't already have the answer. When you ask your teenage daughter, "Why didn't you take out the trash?" there's little sense of curiosity in your question. You are not really curious about the answer. You just want to challenge your daughter for not doing her chores. A similar situation arises when you ask a subordinate, "Why didn't you get that project done on time?" or "Why did you make that absurd decision?"

Now, there could be genuine curiosity when you ask the above questions of a subordinate, and the employee will be able to tell by your tone whether or not you really care about the answer. People can justify their actions by asking these kinds of closed, rather than creative and open, questions. There may be times when such questions are absolutely appropriate, but they are not the topic of this book. We're talking about questions that are rooted in curiosity for the purpose of learning and benefiting from the answer.

A whole range of questions can be asked if you have a clear point of view and a definite end point in mind. What we're suggesting is that if you can maintain a mindset of genuine curiosity rather than thinking, "I know what has to happen here," you open up a new set of possibilities.

Consider the example of Thomas Edison. When he put the first filament in a light bulb, it didn't work. He could have said, "Okay, that didn't work, so I'm done." Or he could have said, "Let's see if I can learn something from this. I wonder what else I might try." He went through a very rigorous process of continually asking himself questions about what he could do differently. Then, after many tests (sixteen hundred different materials, to be exact), he found one that worked. Our approach to using real questions is closely linked to the scientific method of exploring, forming a hypothesis, and testing it.

Now, we're *not* suggesting that a leader look at his team and say, "I have no idea what we're doing. I certainly don't know where to go. What do you think?" Instead, we suggest that it's the leader's job to establish the North Star for the team through the kind of reflection and self-questioning we talked about in the last chapter. Once he's established those ground rules and determined a desired outcome or goal, he can say, "This is the direction we're taking." He can then ask questions that help the team jointly explore multiple ways to reach the goal.

Examples of open questions might be:

1. What do you (the team) think would happen competitively if we were to change our products?

2. What has happened in the past when we tried to raise prices?

3. What changes in our supply chain can we make to enhance our margin?

It's all about different questions to fit different situations. No matter what the circumstances are, we always must begin with the deliberate attitude of the leader. Does he have a Knower mindset or a Learner mindset?

There are too many managers today whose default is the Knower mindset. Their questions don't lead to a place of open possibility. Their questions feel closed, judgmental, and restrictive. Instead of opening the conversation to potentialities, they actually cap the potential of any conversation, be it in a team meeting or a one-on-one exchange.

GUY'S POKER CHIP EXERCISE

When I work with executives, I encourage them to pause and ask creative, curious questions rather than give orders. I often ask them to indulge in what I call "the poker chip exercise." They are told that they get to start their morning with five poker chips in their right pocket. Whenever they give a directive, as opposed to asking an open question based on genuine curiosity, or whenever they just start telling people what to do, I ask them to move a chip from their right to their left pocket. I say, "Just start with five poker chips and see how far into the day you get before your pocket is empty." They invariably call me before 10:00 a.m. to say, "I'm already out of chips!" Leaders are practiced at giving orders and pushing other people with their answers; they aren't used to pausing and questioning. The exercise creates a surprising self-awareness of their leadership style.

I suggest that you apply this exercise to your own day and track your ratio of the real questions you ask to orders or declarations that you make. Keep track of one week's results, and, in the next week, attempt to create a real shift by upping the percentage of authentic questions you ask. This technique has been adapted from Liz Wiseman's book *Multipliers*.

WHAT MAKES GREAT QUESTIONS?

There are several key elements to keep in mind when forming open, curious questions. They must be authentic and genuine. That means the speaker is searching honestly for new ideas and doesn't have a predetermined set of answers or a very narrow goal in mind. Questions allow people to leave behind some of their own preconceived notions and encourage them to think in ways they had not thought previously.

Truly great questions expand the "sandbox," the place where the team is allowed to play. They make people reconsider some of the assumptions under which they often labor, such as, "We can't do that because we don't have enough financial resources," or "We can't do that because we don't have enough people," or, our favorite, "Our customers won't let us do that." When you question old ways of thinking, you open up opportunities for the team to learn and solve problems in new ways.

To ask questions that challenge assumptions, you have to understand people's current assumptions and limiting thoughts. You can begin to discover this propensity by asking questions that allow people to explore and brainstorm at the edges of where they are, and possibly into the future or even off on the horizon.

Great questions avoid the appearance of blame. Say somebody got hurt on a factory floor, and the team leader is coming in to explore the circumstances. He has to avoid, as his first question, "How could this happen and who did it?" That sort of an opening bombardment will just shut people down or prompt them to justify what they've done. On the other hand, if he asks, "How can we be sure this doesn't ever happen again?" he'll get a very different kind of response. People can join with him in finding an answer, and they could end up with a new approach to keeping the work environment safe.

What we're trying to do is get people to focus on the future rather than on who is to blame. Far too quickly, blame turns to shame, which makes people feel very disempowered instead of feeling like part of a solution, ready to move forward to a resolution. One of most celebrated TED talks we have ever experienced was delivered by Dr. Brené Brown, who wrote *Daring Greatly*. She talked about the power of blame and shame and how it shuts us down. The beauty of this discussion is that you can avoid going anywhere near those negative feelings where productivity decreases and dissatisfaction increases. When that negative response is promoted, you push the culture to be closed and defensive. You can avoid that contagion by asking open questions stemming from genuine curiosity. (We strongly encourage you to watch Brené's TED talk, *The Power of Vulnerability*).

ALLAN ON QUESTIONS OF A PROFESSIONAL COACH

In the professional coaching world, a great question comes down to two words: what and how. When we ask a "what" or "how" question from a place of curiosity, we're essentially creating a learning environment that invites the client to look to the truth and respond in a conversational way; simply stated, avoid all the yes-or-no questions.

"Did you change the oil in the car?" Yes. End of conversation. We don't know about the quality of the oil, when you changed it, or what it cost. Instead, you might ask, "How was your experience when you took the car to get the oil changed?" You can just imagine the different kinds of information you might get if you asked the question that way.

When talking about team performance, a typical leader might ask, "Why did we miss our targets last month?" As coaches, we wouldn't ask that because it takes the conversation to a place where people justify what happened and many generate excuses. That kind of conversation probably isn't going to offer a great deal of new information that we can use to improve the situation. Instead, we could ask, "What could we have done differently to achieve our targets?" An alternative might be, "What didn't we do that might have made a difference?"

From a professional coaching perspective, the purpose of a question is to either deepen the client's understanding of a subject or to drive the action toward what the client wants. When a coach asks a "what" or a "how" question from a place of curiosity, it allows for new possibility thinking. It allows you to look at something in a new way and consider what you could have done differently to achieve greater results.

Notice during the course of a day how often you are leading with "what" or "how" questions versus "yes/no" questions.

THE QUESTION PYRAMID

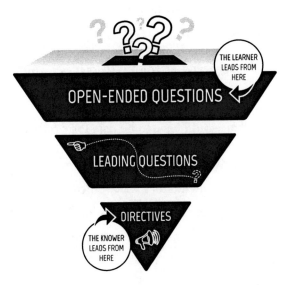

At the top of the inverted pyramid are open-ended questions, the type we've been discussing. As you move towards the bottom of the inverted pyramid, it gets narrower, and the questions become more and more closed and limiting.

At the very bottom of the inverted pyramid are not questions at all, but directive statements such as, "Run for the doors!" At the next level up are questions for which the answer is already known. The question is being asked merely to make someone step up and accept blame. These are questions such as "Who did it?" and "How did you allow this to happen?"

The top of the inverted pyramid presents examples of completely open-ended questions, like:

⇨ "How can we maximize our position?"

⇨ "How can we make sure that such and such won't happen again?

⇨ "What needs attention to achieve your desired outcome?"

⇨ "What would have to be true for x to happen?"

There are certainly circumstances where time or other considerations make it mandatory that someone uses questions from the bottom of the inverted pyramid. If there's a fire in a theater or a boats is sinking, you don't want to say, "How are you feeling about what's going on here?" Not only will that question not help, it's irresponsible.

There will always be circumstances when leaders need to give direction and simply make things happen. What we're suggesting is that finding additional occasions to ask open questions that stem from a genuine sense of curiosity will allow leaders to maximize the future for themselves and their team. We place the open questions at the top of the inverted pyramid because we want them to be used most often, whereas orders or closed questions are used only occasionally.

THE ART OF ASKING QUESTIONS

We all know that communication is made up of the words we use, our tonality, and our body language. A big part of asking artful questions is to consider what is beyond the words.

If there's a breakdown in communication when we're asking questions, we need to explore not only the words that are spoken, but the way in which they are spoken (tonality) and our posture (body language) when we're speaking. We may fail to influence people with our words because our nonverbal cues indicate closed thinking, particularly if we have a Knower mindset. The *words* may have been spoken, but they don't *feel* inviting and open. When that happens, the people being interrogated may get scared and intimidated and begin to close down. That condition has a real impact in today's world because, as we said, we need everyone in the conversation. When we shift to the Learner mindset and have the right language and nonverbal cues to accompany the exploration, the magic happens.

There's a sequence for asking open, inquisitive questions. First, you have to understand the context. Second, you have to make sure your tone and other nonverbal signals support what you're trying to do. Finally, you ask the right question.

People often think about these things in the reverse order. They open with a question with little or no context, and their tone and body language don't encourage participants to explore or jointly resolve a situation.

The art of asking the great question is a combination of thinking and performing. It's about understanding your purpose, context, and audience (which is why you first spend time reflecting), and then forming a question and asking it with the right tone and posture. If you pound your fist on the table while asking a question, you are going to get a very different result than if you ask the same question while turning up both your palms. The content of the question is the main thing, but if it's not delivered in the right way, it won't work. Learner leadership allows you to be conscious of both what and how you communicate.

TONALITY

As the saying goes, "It isn't what you say, but how you say it." This difference can make or break a conversation. The tone you want to strike is one that makes your audience feel you're coming at the conversation from the same side of the desk. It's a *we* orientation versus a *me* and a *you*. It's a solution-based system versus a problem-based process. It's inviting and non-threatening. People, particularly millennials, are listening for the invitation to be a part of the conversation. When you're stressed, the right words might come out, but the invitation should be, for example, "What do you think we can do to get from here to there?" You should avoid, "What are *you* going to do to get this done?"

INFLECTION

Years ago, Allan worked for TMI North America, an international consulting firm focused on creating compelling service cultures. One of the examples in their service program described how a shift of inflection or an emphasis on one word in a sentence can totally change the context. Often, the quality of the inflection in our tone of voice has a significant impact on the listener.

"*I* didn't tell Elizabeth you were lazy."

(Bob did.)

"I *didn't* tell Elizabeth you were lazy."

(It is not true that I told Elizabeth.)

"I didn't *tell* Elizabeth you were lazy."

(I e-mailed her.)

"I didn't tell *Elizabeth* you were lazy."

(I told John, Tom, and Carol.)

"I didn't tell Elizabeth *you* were lazy."

(I said Tom was.)

"I didn't tell Elizabeth you *were* lazy."

(You still are.)

"I didn't tell Elizabeth you were *lazy*."

(You are casual about your work, but not lazy.)

BODY LANGUAGE

What your body is saying may or may not be in line with your words. Staying calm and keeping eye contact will help you invite people into the conversation. Otherwise, people sense a disconnection. This is elementary to the human condition. When someone looks at you the wrong way, you think, "Gosh, what did I do?"

Obviously, fists on tables indicate declarations even if there are questions being asked. But turned-up and outstretched palms—either one or both—invite people into the discussion. An arm waved in a soft, open arc indicates, "I'm with you and we're exploring." Arms that are held in, or even worse, folded, indicate the speaker is closed. Some people are born frowners; others are natural smilers. We all need to take responsibly for how we posture when we're in this kind of situation.

CONTEXT

The context is about what's happening right here and now; it's also about putting yourself in other people's shoes and understanding how they're affected by what's happening. You can ask a question, and it will mean one thing in an environment where things are going well, and something else entirely if things have gone poorly. This difference has to do with your audience's frame of mind. Are your listeners in a positive mode or a worried mode? Obviously, asking, "How are things going?" to a group of people who just experienced a 20 percent layoff is quite different from presenting the same question to a group who just exceeded its sales goals for the quarter.

This arena is where empathy, trust, and intent become important. If a leader can be empathetic, that will come across positively. On the other hand, if the person you're talking to doesn't trust you, it's very hard to get the conversation going in the right direction. Many professional coaches suggest starting off a conversation by assuming positive intent. If you come in with positive intentions, the conversation will move ahead very differently and much more rapidly than if you assume negative intent.

Ask yourself:

1. Is there something about you or your position that might color your interaction?

2. What's your past history with these people?

3. What's happened today? What circumstances might affect people?

4. Do you naturally assume positive or negative intent when you approach a situation?

DOS AND DON'TS

1. Ask open-ended questions that start with "What ..." and "How ..." rather than yes or no questions.

2. Notice your mindset (is it open or closed?) before you speak. Do you already have your own answer to the question you're asking, or are you open to discussion?

3. Ask questions that give people permission to break out of the box or old models and encourage thinking about new possibilities.

4. Pause before engaging and take enough time to learn the facts and issues before you discuss.

5. Try to get a good mix of people with relevant backgrounds and opinions involved in brainstorming.

1. Ask a question that assigns blame or guilt.

2. Let a team brainstorm on a topic about which you, as the leader, have already made up your mind.

3. Come to a meeting without a desired outcome in mind that you have communicated to the team or individual involved in the meeting.

4. Rush into a conversation without having paused to reflect on what you need to know before engaging.

5. Engage in possibility thinking and/or brainstorming on a topic when it is clear to you that you cannot fix the issue.

CLASSIC QUESTIONS THROUGH TIME

John F. Kennedy said, "Ask not what your country can do for you, but what you can do for your country." The statement was meant as a question of purpose, and was offered up as a call to action. It exemplifies what we're talking about because:

- Kennedy didn't have the answer. He wasn't telling people they should volunteer for the Peace Corp or help achieve a successful moon landing. It was a genuine question.

- It implies a we, not a me, mentality. It's our country and we can all do something to move it forward. He invited people to participate in whatever way they could.

- It helped people break the rules. Normally, citizens assume the president works for them. JFK's question stretched the boundaries of what we typically consider when we think about citizenship.

- The question was an inviting and inspiring call to action.

IMAGINE THE IMPACT ON OUR WORLD IF ...

Rosa Parks hadn't asked herself,
"Why can't I sit in the front of the bus?"

Steve Jobs hadn't asked,
"Is there a more user-friendly computer
experience that can be created?"

Adolph Rickenbacker, who
invented the electric guitar, hadn't asked,
"What if I could amplify the sound on a guitar?"

Well-delivered questions rarely pop out of our mouths without thought. In summary, before we move to the next chapter, it is vital to realize the importance of forging questions through preparation, reflection, and curiosity—a deliberate process which allows you to ask the kind of question that will amplify results.

CHAPTER 4

Activating the Learner Mindset

A psychiatrist friend once explained to Guy that in order for the brain to be ready to learn, it needs to be stimulated to a certain extent, but not over stimulated. Studies done on mice show that if they are overstressed, the mice will stop learning. In other words, a bit of excitement gets them to learn, and a little more gets them to learn more, but too much excitement decreases their ability to learn. The idea here is that you want your brain to be in the right gear, which is why you take a moment to reflect before acting or asking questions. You don't want to be in an over stimulated or reactive mode, but rather one in which you're saying to yourself, "Hey, I'm in control, and I'm going to put some thoughtful effort into this situation."

Daniel Kahneman, in his book, *Thinking Fast and Slow*, makes the point that if you allow your fast-thinking brain to take control, you can make all kinds of mistakes. What you want to do instead is to set up the brain to grab control and activate that Learner mindset so you're not on autopilot; you're purposefully achieving your goals.

So how do you ensure success in this process? How do you put the Learner mindset into action? What does it mean to become activated? In Chapter 2 we focused on the internal mindset, where the set point is for the individual, and how to reflect in order establish that internal readiness. Now we're shifting to how to activate that mindset.

> Ask yourself how often you are
> on autopilot in your role at work.

A SENSE OF WONDER AND AWE

You have paused and reflected. You are grounded. Now you can initiate some structured thinking which activates your Learner mindset. As a Learner, you are willing to explore the edges of what you do know and do not know. Your goal is to turn on the curiosity and wonder in your brain.

We use the word *wonder* because curiosity can seem a bit flat for what we're trying to describe. You might be curious about a fact or a detail, but what we really want people to say is, "I wonder what if . . ." and "I wonder how . . ." There's a deepening, an expansiveness, when you talk about wonder. It has an open, childlike feel, with few limitations on your thinking, few restrictions limited by past experience or even assumptions. What you're really trying to do by activating the Learner mindset is to turn on that internal sense of wonder and then help turn it on in others. (In the next chapter, we'll talk about what you can do to orient your team or audience to the same way of thinking.) Sharing this wonder is, in a sense, what Walt Disney did.

When people are in this state of mind, the traditional boundaries of seniority, roles, and rigid social structures disappear. When everybody's looking at the sky in a sense of wonder, they're not thinking about who the boss is and who the employer is. They are truly on the same side of the table because they're peers in what they're exploring.

A leader certainly has some responsibilities that are different from followers, but the truth is that, when we're being creative and curious, we're all equals. A leader's humility can help create that sense of creative wonder, which allows everyone to move forward and think differently about a given circumstance. When that leader is in the Learner mindset, something wonderful happens. We've said before: It's like a positive virus. Status evaporates. Hierarchy evaporates. The differentials evaporate. All of a sudden, you're in this place of incubation, where everyone is focused on finding solutions and possibilities.

HOW TO ACTIVATE YOUR LEARNER MINDSET

There are specific actions you can take to get yourself ready for broader thinking. The following are three things you can do to activate your Learner mindset.

1. Challenge Your Assumptions

Start by looking at the assumptions you bring to a situation. Push the edge of those assumptions to see if they're real, or if they're just things that you've quietly or tacitly agreed to, only to find that they have narrowed your potential.

COMMON BUSINESS ASSUMPTIONS

Assumptions lock our thinking. Understanding the risk helps break the bonds. Jim Luckman of the Lean Transformations Group has distilled his years of work with leadership assumptions into the following categories:

1. Results thinking (*versus* means thinking): Leaders focus on results, believing that paying attention to them will create action by the people who achieve results; for example, focusing on monthly sales instead of sales appointments.

2. Fragmented thinking (versus systems thinking): We tend to break things apart to better understand and control our systems. Organizations are broken into parts to better control the functions of the company. For example, the purchasing department seeks low-cost parts without regard to the problems in quality or delivery that may surface later.

3. Control thinking (versus adaptive thinking): Managers and leaders often believe they need to control their people. They think that if they could simply control a certain function, the system would improve.

4. Defensive thinking (versus internalization thinking): Often, a manager's initial response to a problem is to decide whom to blame. For example, parents are suing Google, claiming that the company made it too easy for their children to buy apps. A more immediate and effective way to address the problem would be for the parents to first examine their own behavior and their relationship with their children.

When business leaders fail to question these assumptions, they cannot break through to new levels of performance in their organization because they shut down organizational thinking. The act of questioning assumptions creates energy and has been demonstrated to achieve significant engagement and increased performance.

Guy once worked with a hospital team that was responsible for processing pathology results. They'd take a small sample of tissue and put it in a machine to process overnight. At eight in the morning, the staff returned to start working on the samples. They'd finish by two or three in the afternoon when the doctor would assess the samples for cancer. By the time physical determination occurred, it was too late to get the patient an answer until the following day. When we organized a team meeting at the hospital, we found that all the team members felt terrible because the process took two full days, which, for patients who were nervous about having cancer, seems a long time to wait for results.

The team members wished they could get the results back faster, but they were locked into this mindset that the process had to take two days. Then, very quietly, someone got up the nerve to speak. She said, "You know, if I could start at 4:00 a.m., I could have the work done by 8:00 a.m., and we could have the diagnosis to the patient by noon. Then we could get patients their results in just one day."

The group said, "Oh, that's a great idea, except it can't happen because 1) the entire hospital starts up at eight in the morning, and 2) most people in pathology take public transport, and public transport doesn't start that early." People could only see the constraints, so they were about to give up when the leader of the group said, "Well, *what would happen if* I could make parking passes available to pathology people who wanted to start at 4:00 a.m.?" The whole group looked at each other and started thinking. Then, people said, "Yes, but who really wants to that start early?" All of a sudden, hands started going up. They had more people offering to start early than they needed.

No one had considered that, for lifestyle reasons, some people would love to get to work at 4:00 a.m. and finish their day at 1:00 p.m., so they could have the rest of the day for their kids or other priorities. Asking "What would happen if . . . ?" changed everything. They were able to get pathology answers within 24 hours, which was a huge benefit to patients. Pretty soon, the entire organization was talking about how the leader had broken the rules by getting parking passes for "regular people," which led them to start thinking differently about their purpose and values. And all because of some creative questions that were asked about a work system. If you have a prepared mind, if you're ready to think differently and challenge assumptions, you can move much further forward than you might have thought.

> Ask yourself what your assumptions are about the current circumstance. Explore and push the edges of those assumptions.

2. Bring in Fresh Eyes

The second technique for activating a Learner mindset is to involve what we call fresh eyes—that is, outside people who have a different point of view, or, equally important, customers who are receivers of the work. It's amazing what can happen when you listen to outside people who don't know all the rules and haven't been soaked in your work tradition. They're willing to think completely differently about problems and solutions.

Bringing fresh eyes to a situation can activate a creative Learner mindset because the last one to see water is the goldfish. When you're in the goldfish bowl, everything looks fine. You don't notice you're in water.

In Allan's first book, *Bold Moves*, one of the things he and his coauthor talked about was the fact that when people are ready to make a bold move, they have to recognize that sometimes it's a team sport. Inviting other perspectives can lead to results that go way beyond what was ever considered possible.

There are a lot of leaders out there who feel they have to figure it all out themselves. Allan challenges leaders to establish a board of advisors—an advisory team—to which they have access maybe three or four times a year. The people on this board are not controlling the leader's paycheck. They're not involved with his job, but they care about his success and bring a different perspective.

It's helpful to recognize that there are times when we're not meant to go it alone. We've got to get those fresh eyes to broaden our perspective, to bring in some outside thinking, to challenge some of our assumptions, and to help us move forward.

A project on which Guy consulted, with a hospital group, illustrates the value fresh eyes can bring to the whole team. The group had been looking at the patient experience of children. They had been through several workshops to improve their registration process and other mechanical aspects of a patient's arrival at and passage through the hospital, but then they ran out of areas to improve. They thought they were in pretty good shape, until we brought in two mothers who had "frequent flier children," kids with chronic illnesses who visited the hospital regularly.

The tone of the entire workshop shifted when these patients came in. The mothers said, "If you think painted butterflies on the wall make a family-friendly environment, you're crazy. You should be thinking about the fact that children want to see other kids. They don't want to see a roomful of children who look obviously sick. So can we change the sight lines in the room, so we're not looking at every single patient in the waiting room? And we'd like you to change the games and other things you have to engage the kids because what you've got are, frankly, terrible."

Both mothers were fabulous with their creative ideas and their willingness to speak boldly to senior hospital leaders. They weren't being negative. They just said, "No one's ever asked us, and we've got so much to tell you." Many work processes are designed to feed a customer with what we think they want, instead of getting real answers from the customers themselves.

3. Involve the Group

A third technique is to have that fresh-eye conversation by means of a group, rather than a one-on-one discussion. The Knower might use the idea of gaining another perspective in a one-on-one interview. He'll gather a bunch of facts and come to a conclusion on his own. By doing it that way, the outcomes are limited by 1) the leader's ideas, and 2) the nature of a one-on-one dialogue.

A Learner leader, who's not trying to control the situation or own the outcome, will bring a group of people together and create an active dialogue. What happens is that participants start feeding off each other. The set of ideas people come up with expands. One small comment gets amplified by a second person, and it zooms out much further than it ever would have in a series of one-on-one interviews. The whole thing just amplifies itself, like a deeply-resonating drum.

4. Be Open to the Answers

When you ask questions in a Learner mindset, you are open to other people's answers and even open to the fact that people's answers and ideas may be better than your own. These techniques are part and parcel of respecting others and what they have to offer.

Guy once encountered a bright, strong-willed department leader who shut down every idea or suggestion that touched on her work area during the value stream mapping session that he was leading. For the first time in 15 years of guiding teams, Guy thought he would have to ask her to leave. Instead, her took her aside and had a private discussion, during which they agreed she could stay if she would only ask questions and make no assertions. In short, it worked out beautifully. She finished the day with a big smile and the team achieved significant improvements. The other leaders of the group even came up to Guy afterward and thanked him for the intervention. Asking questions in the right frame of mind is powerful.

MAPPING AS A TOOL FOR ELIMINATING HIERARCHY

In Guy's process improvement workshops, he often uses a mapping exercise to help individuals better understand problems and work flow. A lot of people who have done mapping before think the goal of the exercise is to create a detailed diagram. What they don't understand is that when everybody in the group looks at the same map and puts shared marks on it, what they're really doing is making themselves peers and colleagues and erasing all their corporate boundaries. The creation of the map creates a horizontal team of people, all looking at the same work, which starts to eliminate that sense of hierarchy. It shows that everyone is respected because everyone has a pen in hand and equal power to erase, add, and change things. When that openness occurs, the creative ideas just start to fly. The real purpose and value of the mapping session is to create a shared vision for the future.

Interestingly, Knower- and Learner-oriented personalities can work very effectively together when using a visual, shared map as the basis for discussion.

GUY ON ASKING DIFFERENT QUESTIONS

I was once at a dinner with four entrepreneurs who were talking about how best to get new employees on board and up to speed. In a funny way, I felt like a dinosaur as the conversation got started because my mind and comments were focused on all the traditional things, such as getting the right badges, new e-mail addresses, and desks—all the things people need in their first days of work.

The four leaders at the table almost laughed at me. They said, "You really don't get it at all. Our worry is not about hiring people and making them productive. That task we're sure we can accomplish. Our worry is about how we can get employees to be such raging fans of the company that they bring some of their friends to join us, because our biggest problem is finding talent. What we're thinking about is the exciting, positive things we can do, such as having a social gathering at the end of the first day for the new employee so she's really celebrated, or writing, "Welcome Stephanie," on the corner of every white board in the building, or having a catered dinner sent home so that when that person gets home from work, not only is she excited, but her family says, "What kind of place is this?"'

What they were doing was thinking about the problem in a very different way. They were asking questions about how to make someone a raging fan, instead of how to make productive employees pay for themselves. In doing that, they were really modeling all of the ideas that we've presented so far. They were breaking the mental model (assumption) of the employee as a producer for the company. They were turning that around. "No," they said. "An employee is on board with us to help us find other great employees." And the only way for this to work was to come at the question in a creative way.

A FOCUS ON PAST, PRESENT, AND FUTURE
WITH RESPECT AND HUMILITY

Consider this concept: *reflecting* is focused on the past; *inspecting* is focused on the present; and *expecting* is focused on the future that we're going to design together. In any event, you must undertake all of the above rules with a sense of respect by entering into the situation with a sense of humility for the team and what they can do that you can't do alone. Together, in a creative and open-minded way, you build your understanding of the history and key assumptions and ask all the questions you can about the current situation, which is how you arrive at a new place together.

The inspection part of the process is about recognizing all of the facts of the situation. If you don't have all the facts, then future decisions could be limited or even wrong. To really inspect a situation, you should think about whether you need outside data and/or outside expertise, and you should understand all the current facts and assumptions with which you're working. Once you have all available facts and assumptions, you can really dig in and brainstorm.

When we talk about *expecting*, we're really talking about figuring out what we want to happen, what it will look like, when it will get done, and who will be responsible for it. In many ways, expecting is where accountability comes into play. This is where we activate that action plan and then circle back and ask, "How did our results compare with our plan?"

The reason this last part is so important is that we see lots of teams that are really good at having open-spirited brainstorming conversations, but can't come up with a good answer when we circle back and say, "What happened to that idea we talked about a month ago?" We find that nobody pulled those ideas back to the practical and tactical. To ask people for their best ideas and then lose them in the ether is to disrespect others. Setting expectations and being tight and clear about what we want to achieve, when we want to achieve it, and who's going to be actively engaged in getting it done is a fundamental part of respecting other people's time, effort, and ideas.

GO SEE, ASK WHY, SHOW RESPECT

Mr. Cho, who was the long-standing chairman of Toyota, was once asked, "What is lean leadership?" Lean is the set of management ideas that Toyota has used to make work better in many different ways, and the reason why Toyota is such a powerful global company. Mr. Cho's answer was the simple, three-phrase statement, or mantra, "Go see, ask why, show respect."

That model is exactly what we're talking about when the proper mindset is activated. When Mr. Cho says, "Go see," what he means is, "Go and gather real facts, not filtered stories through reports or formal presentations. Go to where the work gets done and talk to the people who do the actual work. Really dig in."

Now, there are managers who wander cubicles, looking for people who are doing something wrong, but they are not our role models. That kind of "going to see" shuts down people's creative thinking and causes them to put up barriers. What we're trying to *do* is create a learning opportunity in which everybody participates and expands his or her knowledge; not just of how to do things but also how *not to do things*. Again, humility and respect have to be the foundation here, or you don't have the standing to ask questions and drill in deeper because drilling in deeper in a positive way makes everyone feel good, but if it's not positive, it makes people feel blamed.

"Ask why" is shorthand for turning on your creative mind and asking broad, open-spirited questions. Mr. Cho used the word *why*. There's a technique in the continuous improvement world called the five whys (which you can read more about online if you're interested), but it's not really about the question of why. It's about asking evermore probing questions.

The third piece of the mantra is "Show respect." You're showing respect by 1) asking the people who do the work what the situation is, 2) asking those same people about the future and potential of their work, and 3) supporting and helping them achieve a new way of getting that work done.

Mr. Cho modeled this idea with his respect for facts, for learning, and for people. When you put the pieces of the mantra together, you become a Learner leader, not a Knower who just throws answers at problems.

ALLAN ON THE IMPORTANCE OF RESPECT IN COMMUNICATION

For years, I've run a communications exercise in which participants take a short quiz to determine which of four communications styles feels right to them. The four styles are: the logical style; the questioning, fact-finder style; the cheerleading style; and the humble, easy-to-get-along-with, team-player style. Basically, I say to each group, "Once you've determined your type, please write down how you'd like people to communicate with you." In the 20 years I've been doing this exercise, there's one word that always shows up regardless of which communication style people identify with. That word is respect. Everyone wants to be treated with respect. And yet, so often, respect gets lost in an exchange and the whole conversation begins to crumble. When respect falls out—and we've all experienced this—people, psychologically, withdraw from the conversation. They may give you visual clues that they're still engaged, but they're not.

WHY ARE RESPECT AND HUMILITY SO IMPORTANT IN THE WORKPLACE?

The thing about respect and humility is that they can't be faked. They require the Learner leader to come from a very transparent and authentic place in order to engage, which is why we talk about authentic or genuine questions being key. Once the Learner mindset is activated, when these questions come through, people know they're genuine and earnest. They can sense it in a heartbeat, and, if they get that kind of question, they immediately give back. It's almost like a gift. The leader gives others the respect of not coming in with preconceived notions or answers, and people immediately give back by putting their very best thoughts and efforts into the endeavor.

In today's environment, where employees feel much more mobile and much less emotionally tied to a business, respect and humility become ever more important for employee retention and for encouraging employees' best efforts. There's a very different mindset behind having a job in order to collect some cash, and having a job in which you feel connected. When you put your heart and soul into the business and share creative energy to help the business grow and go someplace new—powerful results occur. It's becoming harder and harder to create that kind of loyalty and investment in today's workforce. Leading with respect and humility is really an opportunity to improve employee engagement and corporate stability, which will anchor the business so it can grow and get where it needs to be.

In order to create the kind of culture in which people want to be invested, you've got to start with earnestness, honesty, and genuineness in yourself. You've got to activate the Learner mindset in yourself before you can activate it in others. Only then will the questions you chew on together be accepted and eagerly debated in a creative, open-spirited way. This new spirit leads to bigger and better outcomes for all.

CHAPTER 5

Leading Knowers and Learners

T he purpose of this chapter is to prepare you to lead different types of people. You may have team members who are predominately Learners and others who are predominately Knowers. What will you do differently to lead them? We'll talk about leading both types, as well as how to put thought into action, because new ideas mean nothing if you don't act on them.

When we think about the difference between leading Knowers and Learners, we think about skiing. Anyone who skis knows that if you lean back, which may be your natural impulse, then your skis will shoot out in front of you and you will have much less control. The key is to lean forward and stay balanced over the top of your skis, even if it feels unnatural at first. Knowers can be so eager to stay in control that they tend to lean back, to pull back to what they know, even though they understand that is not the best way to proceed. As a leader, if you have Knowers on your team, your task is to pull them forward, to get them balanced on top of their skis.

Learners often have the opposite impulse. While Knowers tend to lean too far back, Learners can lean too far forward. And if you lean too far forward, past the tips of your skis, you risk going too fast and taking a tumble. Learners can sometimes get so excited about what's out in front of them that their ideas and plans get too far beyond others in the group or the real constraints of the organization.

As a leader, whether you have Learners or Knowers on your team, it's important to help your people stay centered and balanced. The gift that Learner leaders have is being able to walk into a room and know who's who. They can see who is leaning forward and curious, and who is hanging back. And when they see those differences, they can figure out how best to help each individual move forward with balance.

As a Learner leader, you should recognize that any situation requiring your attention is an opportunity to engage. It's helpful if you can frame that engagement in your head. The first thing to do is to pause. Then, read the mindset of the people involved to understand whether they are Knowers, Learners, or somewhere in between, so you can address individually their very distinct needs in order to make progress toward your goals.

LEADING KNOWERS

As we've learned, a Knower's energy is more contained, more controlled, and more guarded than a Learner's. Knowers may be pontificating, but their orientation is me focused versus we focused. A Learner leader will be able to spot this critical difference.

You can identify Knowers by observing that their orientation is driven by data and justification, and that they often use assumptions as walls to corral a conversation. To protect their position, they often use facts as bullets and stories as shields. They will fire facts at you so they don't have to rethink something or change their behavior. Then they'll tell stories, because while they're telling stories, they don't have to make the effort to think in a new way. There's often a defensive and distracting energy when someone asks the Knower a question. And when Knowers speak, they tend to speak from a place of false authority. They may sound gruff, unfriendly, even biting. What you're picking up on is their defensiveness because they feel they have to know the answer, be in control, and always look good. That dedication to the wrong emotions takes up a lot of energy in a room.

One way that Knowers can be successful is through the power of control. They shoot out facts and details in a targeted way that shuts individuals down and constrains thought. When this happens, people tend to withdraw because they feel targeted and unsafe. They don't physically leave the room, but they scurry energetically out of the way. Over time, Knowers pick up on the fact that this style allows them to push people aside so they get their own way, but not through popularity or because they have the best ideas.

Knowers may also have a practiced skill whereby they use data and detail to drown out any kind of questioning or probing. Those asking the questions often don't have the same arsenal of data, so they can't fight back. Innovation and creativity just don't happen under these kinds of circumstances. You may be moving through your agenda, but what are you gaining? Where's the curiosity? Where's the innovation when you let someone like that have the microphone?

So what happens when you try to address the Knower? How do you open the door? How do you set the stage so you can move Knowers to a place where they can begin to be curious? Some possible countermeasures for working with Knowers include the following:

1. State clearly that you want to spend time brainstorming what's possible. Consider using the 80/20 rule, which means looking only at the things that happen most often, or 80 percent of the time, because if you can fix the "most oftens," you're mostly better off. You don't

have to have a solution for every possible circumstance that anyone can dream up. You will often hear Knowers say, "This won't work because such-and-such happened years ago," so make it clear up front that that kind of objection isn't relevant to the conversation.

2. Say to Knowers who are using facts to derail the conversation, "I hear all the things you're saying, but what *don't* you know and what don't we know about this circumstance?" You can diffuse the situation by simply saying in a relaxed tone, "Can we talk about the things that are truly unknowns here?" This allows us to put Knowers and Learners on an equal footing in the conversation. If you can play off that, it starts to diffuse the power struggle and presents an opportunity for people to open up their thinking.

THE MANY FACES OF KNOWERS

Knowers exhibit a variety of different characteristics. If you notice one of the following personality types on your team (or identify with one yourself), think about how you can bring that person around to becoming more of a Learner.

The Disconnected

Disconnected people may be nodding at you, but they're not engaged. They're thinking, "Let's get through this foolishness. I've got other things to do. I'm not really invested in this conversation." Their eyes might be looking down at their watch or scanning their e-mail on their hand-held devices. These are the people at a cocktail party who look over your shoulder to see who else is in the room while you attempt to have a conversation with them.

When people are ready to leave a meeting, they often disconnect unconsciously from what's happening. You can see it. They start closing their binders and organizing their things while you're still talking. All these little behaviors—bad behaviors, really—are things we tend to ignore. We can really shift this kind of energy by asking people to put away distractions and focus on what's happening right here, right now. The solution is to move from disconnected to connected.

The key is to notice the disconnection. If you don't have that awareness, there is limited possibility for change. Everyone becomes disconnected at times, even Learner leaders. The important thing is to notice the disconnection and redirect people's attention so they're connected with what's going on.

The Interrupter

Interrupters can't but help but be in charge of the conversation to the point where they interrupt consistently. They believe they add value to the conversation by over talking and blessing everyone with their wisdom. They feel compelled to control the conversation even when someone else initiated the topic. Their egos need to be fed by providing content and speaking with an attitude of, "I know this domain and let me enlighten you." They may be so impassioned that they see the interruption as only a small interference that pales in comparison to the value they believe they're providing. Some will even say, "Sorry for interrupting, but I think that . . . ," and continue to interrupt. The solution is to move from a *me* orientation to a *you* orientation.

Help the interrupter adopt the popular adage of "seek first to understand and then to be understood." This allows him to calibrate his communication style and not interrupt. There are times when one needs to intrude in a conversation for a number of reasons, but the common practice of talking over or interrupting someone is a bad habit that moves one into a Knower mindset—with unfortunate results.

The Critic

We've all seen this personality at work. Critics come to the conversation or meeting in what appears to be a bad mood. Angry, annoyed, and stubborn, their raison d'être, or purpose, seems to be to discover what's wrong with whatever is being discussed. They're wired to be critical and pessimistic and, oftentimes, confuse issues with facts. This negativity stems from a desire to maintain power and control. While there are times when scrupulous attention to detail and a critical eye are needed for a conversation or project, critics arrive at meetings or exchanges with one agenda: to seek out what's wrong with the discussion topic. In doing so, they believe they're adding value, but they don't recognize that this overbearing behavior puts people into a lockdown mode wherein they want to get out of the way as soon as possible. The solution is to move from critical to curious.

If a person's set point is to arrive at every situation with a critical perspective, that person will have a negative impact on others and impede open-spirited dialogue.

Coming from a place of curiosity and authenticity, ask the following questions:

1. What assumption have the critics made about this exchange or meeting? If it is a negative one (e.g., this meeting is a waste of time), consider suggesting they redefine the assumption (e.g., try to look for common ground and speak to desired outcomes that hold value for everybody).

2. Ask critics to focus on the shared goals, with a desire to collaborate effectively for a mutually beneficial win.

3. Finally, on the sidelines, ask the critic to notice their mood: What are their emotions as they think about the exchange or meeting? On the continuum between the Knower and Learner mindset, their emotional state is key. What has to occur for the critic to shift their emotional state so they arrive in a better, open mood of curiosity for a richer exchange?

GUY ON PRACTICE MAKES LEARNERS

Over the past 15 years, I've been leading groups in process change efforts, and one of the core techniques we use is something called a value stream map. People draw a map of a current work system, which we call the "current state," and then they draw a map of the "future state" they're proposing, which is the way the same system will work after the proposed changes are made.

We then invite senior leaders to hear the team present the current state and why it's broken, and their vision of how they'd like to fix it, with a rough, high-level diagram. What the team is doing is asking permission from the executives to turn their vision into a 90-day action plan.

Over the course of many years of leading team mapping workshops, I've discovered that executives, when reviewing the work of subordinates, will spend most of their time looking for flaws and pointing out problems in their subordinates' work. It seems that the basic leadership operating assumption is to demonstrate authority by pointing out flaws in other people's work. Most executives must be prompted by the coach or team leader to look at the quality of the ideas presented and to not look for small flaws. We guide them on how to ask thoughtful questions about the work and the team's vision for the future.

It's been absolutely fascinating to see how difficult this process is for many executives, who, for their entire professional lives, have been able to look quickly at numbers and show something is wrong. The key point here is that asking thoughtful questions is truly a learned skill that takes some practice. You need to try it more than once before you can really understand how to sit back and look at systems from a high-level viewpoint instead of worrying about fine-grained facts and details. The opportunity is to then ask open questions that take the conversation forward rather than just giving orders, finding flaws, or telling people, "No." Some of our worst outcomes occur when an uninformed senior leader walks in and says, "That'll never work." The minute a leader articulates that language, the work of the team goes right out the window. It's really important that leaders learn to pause before they speak and respond through questions instead of declarations, so they can open up, instead of shut down, the thinking of the people they lead.

Ask yourself how often, when you spot Knower behavior in a meeting, you try to redirect that energy rather than just letting it go.

LEADING LEARNERS

When you're leading Learners, there's a very different kind of energy. There's an openness and a leaning toward what's possible. We all love to work with positive energy, but enthusiasm also, sometimes, has to be corralled. Learners get excited about big ideas for the future, and you have to help them by setting some guardrails so they stay focused. You have to make sure there's some practicality to their ideas, something you can take action on in the immediate future.

Two specific things you can do to help keep Learners focused are 1) create a specific problem statement that defines your sandbox, and 2) be explicit about what's in and out of scope for the team's challenge. By scope, we mean what items in the business process can be changed, and how broad your authority is to make changes. Hosting a thoughtful conversation about a possible change that leadership, ultimately, will not accept is worse than not having the conversation at all.

Learners may be a bit easier to lead than Knowers, but the core idea for both groups is to think carefully about their assumptions. For Knowers, you want to try not to focus too much on those assumptions. For Learners, you want to help them keep some of those assumptions in mind so you can direct their energy to a common goal.

PUTTING THOUGHT INTO ACTION

Once people have formed new ideas, the next layer to consider is what you can do to get them to bring the ideas to completion. The generation of new ideas will be wasted unless all of you, together, can make something new happen.

As we've said before, when you're in the Learner mindset, you're fostering an environment of curiosity and new possibilities, but you should always be doing so against an agenda or goal. You're not just brainstorming for the sake of the brainstorm. You have an anchor, which is your desired outcome, and it's the leader's responsibility in a learning environment to recognize how much of the conversation is moving you toward that desired outcome. There comes a time when the Learner leader has to say, "Let's now lock down this brainstorming and look at ways to create forward motion for these ideas. What do we want to move forward, who's going to move it forward, and by when?"

One technique that we often use is to put a time box on what the future is so that we can pick the right kinds of changes for the right kind of time window. We've often specified either a month or 90 days to build our action plans. We will not plan beyond 90 days because the speed of business is so fast and people lose interest when they plan too far into the future.

THE RIPPLE EFFECT OF TRANSFORMING KNOWERS

We've mentioned before that people who lead from a Learner mindset affect everyone around them. When those Learner leaders then start actively cultivating Learner behavior in others, the effect is magnified. The entire culture of an organization can shift and amazing things can happen as a result.

In our introduction, we mentioned an executive, Tony, with whom Allan worked for about six months to help him transform from a Knower into a Learner. The transformation was a real success, but what was even more amazing was the ripple effect it had. Not only did Tony get better feedback from his peers and direct reports, but he began to see other areas where his new leadership style had a big impact.

Part of his job was to negotiate union contracts for his company. A situation arose where a nonunion plant suddenly wanted to unionize. Using his old Knower style, he would have adopted a combative response to the situation. But instead, thanks to his new Learner leadership style, he became very curious about why the plant wanted to unionize, so he flew out and sat down with folks on the floor. They had never previously experienced such open management curiosity. When he'd visited the plant previously, he'd only talked to the managers, but now he was out on the shop floor having real conversations about what was happening. He wanted to get a better understanding of what was happening and he wanted to make sure the shop floor workers knew their concerns were heard.

When the plant went to a vote two weeks later, the employees voted not to unionize. He was able to completely shift the plant's culture by demonstrating his genuine interest in the situation and looking at it from the viewpoint of the people who worked there. He began to see how he could have a closer relationship with them so they would feel more valued. And he credited his new leadership style for leading everyone to a mutually positive solution.

Guy witnessed the same kind of transformative effect when working with a very bright and verbal woman who had the job of controller for a financial services firm. She probably fell somewhere in the middle of the Knower versus Learner spectrum, but her habits were all about showing what she knew. At meetings, she would be the first one with the facts on the table, using those facts as bullets to make her argument and make sure other people did what they were supposed to. And, frankly—and she would now agree with this characterization—she would sometimes squelch creative thinking and conversations. By being so good at having facts and information at her fingertips, she would win arguments before she got a chance to learn what the other side was trying to achieve.

She was promoted to CFO, so she moved from a position where she was responsible for lots of fine-grained facts and details to the executive ranks, where her job was more about the overall work system and looking for long-term benefits for the firm. In this new role, she walked into a number of meetings, wearing her old hat. She started closing down conversations with executives, and, all of a sudden, she realized she was hurting herself. So she asked Guy to help her learn how she might behave differently.

One of the things that Guy did was to challenge her to sit in all her meetings over the course of a week and score how often other leaders gave orders instead of asking genuine questions. In doing that, she realized that most of the leaders around her spent their time telling people what to do. Then she and Guy talked about what could be different if she started asking real questions in areas people didn't have hard expertise in, and asking for more clarity on what was going on in those work systems.

She had a wonderful set of successes after that exercise, and a real shift occurred in how she was viewed among her peers. She was asking questions instead of just snapping back with quick answers; this change in attitude caused everyone else to sit back and ponder. From that pondering came discussions about new ideas and things they could do differently. She came to be viewed as a thought leader among her peers, even though she wasn't the one coming up with the thoughts; she was just provoking them. It's a powerful example of how ready people are to adapt to this style of leadership. She realized that her ability to host really unique conversations was, in fact, one of her most valuable contributions to the company.

ROBERT FROST AND THE LEARNER MINDSET

If you know the famous Robert Frost poem, "The Road Not Taken," you can think of the Knower path as the path that's well traveled. It's a path that sticks to those things we already know and with which we are comfortable. The Learner path, on the other hand, is a little scary. It's more open-ended and less traveled. The Learner mindset is, in a way, all about being willing to take the road less traveled and, as the poem says, "that has made all the difference."

The Road Not Taken

Two roads diverged in a yellow wood,
And sorry I could not travel both
And be one traveler, long I stood
And looked down one as far as I could

To where it bent in the undergrowth;
Then took the other, as just as fair,
And having perhaps the better claim,
Because it was grassy and wanted wear;

Though as for that the passing there
Had worn them really about the same,
And both that morning equally lay
In leaves no step had trodden black.

Oh, I kept the first for another day!
Yet knowing how way leads on to way,
I doubted if I should ever come back.
I shall be telling this with a sigh

Somewhere ages and ages hence:
Two roads diverged in a wood, and I—
I took the one less traveled by,
And that has made all the difference.

CHAPTER 6

Setting the Stage

The Bard said, "All the world is a stage..." We ask you to consider the idea that any time you engage with someone, there may be an intentional performance going on. Learner leaders have the skills to create an effective experience for their meetings, which is about more than just finding a room, getting people there, and expecting great outcomes. All too often meetings are scheduled, but the right elements are not in place to ensure a productive outcome. This chapter talks about how to manage different elements in order to set the stage for the best conditions, meaning everybody is leaning in and feeling valued, and really creative thinking happens as a result.

WHEN IS THE BEST TIME TO ACTIVATE
FOR ENHANCED IMPACT?

It's important to understand when to engage the learning mindset and when not to. If you're seated on a plane and the engines go out, that's not the time to jump into a Learner mindset and explore the different options with your fellow passengers. At that moment, it should be heads down, seat belts on—a very directive experience.

If we circle back to the brain science we talked about in Chapter 4, the optimal conditions for learning are when people are stimulated, but not so overly stimulated that their adrenaline is running. Optimum learning comes when we are neither highly emotional, nor functioning on autopilot. The lizard brain takes over when we are too emotional and pops us out of accessing creativity. It's all about timing. Under such circumstances, it's best to say something such as, "Let's wait until tomorrow," or "Let's talk about this in an hour when things calm down."

We talked before about the formal cooling-off periods that people take when they're engaged in intense negotiations. We can do something similar in business by literally calling a time-out to let our emotions calm down and give ourselves a chance to let our front brains, the part responsible for logical and careful thinking, manage the future and keep the goal in mind.

Ask yourself how often you set a time to resolve situations rather than let the situation set the timing for you. Think back to the last three urgent meetings you had. Could you have tackled those problems at a different time for better outcomes?

Another time when we don't want to try to engage in creative thinking is when people are afraid—for themselves—for their careers, for their physical being, or for others. You need first to address the fears that are firing off automatic responses before you can get to a place where creative thinking can take place. Otherwise, you're wasting your time trying to engage in a creative conversation.

When deciding if the timing is right, also consider if there's a requirement for speed. There are circumstances when speed is the primary requirement, and the leader needs to step up and move quickly. To ask people at such a time to pause and be creative is completely inappropriate.

One way to really know when the timing is best is to access your level-three listening, which we'll talk about in the next chapter. Doing so will help the leader know whether or not it's time to activate the Learner mindset for the greatest impact.

STAGING YOUR ENVIRONMENT

Once you know the timing is right, it's important to think about the environment and context of your meeting. All of us have been to the theater or seen a theatrical production, so we know that when we look at a stage, every move, every look, everything, is orchestrated. In a corporate setting, we emulate the director of a play and set the stage to create ripe conditions for amazing meetings and for cultivating that learning mindset.

The only distinction between what we do and the theater is that we are setting the stage to search for an unknown conclusion, not a known conclusion. This is an unusual kind of theater, more like improv theater, because we're not trying to get to an endpoint that's already been written. We're trying to set the stage for people to do genuine, open-spirited, and creative thinking, and to create their own conclusion. This is a unique process; it is not manipulative. It's simply about understanding the ecosystem and creating conditions in which people can bring their very best talents to the topic at hand.

Setting the stage involves managing the following components:

Setting

The topic of setting the stage is interesting, because for decades the environmental setting for meetings and for work was not considered a key element. The workplace environment has traditionally been about process and getting things done, but in the last decade or two, amazing leaders have begun to say, "Wait a minute. If we're in the business of innovation and creation, don't we need to look at the kind of environment that will help us be creative and innovative?"

One of the early game changers in this area was Pixar Animation, the film company in northern California. Pixar was this little bitty company that was producing the most amazing, cutting-edge animated films the world had ever seen. People began to be very curious about how this little company was doing all this.

Pixar had created a work environment that most people had never seen before. In the book *Creativity, Inc.*, authors Ed Catmull and Amy Wallace share how creativity shot through the roof when an open, transparent environment was created, despite the structures that were in place as the company grew. The entire environment had a kind of feel-good creative energy. The management really thought about what their people needed to do to stimulate their best creative thinking. Pixar's tremendous success tells the rest of the story.

We now have many examples of environments like that, particularly within entrepreneurial tech companies. These start-ups provide good spaces and ensured services. They often have aggressive catering and food access. They've got wonderful *ad hoc* meeting rooms. All of this stage-dressing is designed for one purpose: to foster creativity. The point is that companies large and small have recognized that we've given short shrift to our working environments and the different ways in which they can help engage people.

When it comes to the meetings you lead, ask yourself how the environment you choose can help set the right conditions for getting the outcome you want. Ask yourself where the meeting will take place and when it will take place. Will it happen during normal business hours, or during off hours? Maybe it will take place on a Saturday morning, offsite? Maybe it will take place at a dinner? Or maybe it will be in a typical conference room? These kinds of considerations should be part of your thinking when you're planning your meeting. You want a place that will encourage those Learner attributes to come alive. If you're sitting in a meeting room on the building's windowless, subterranean floor and you're participating in an eight-hour innovation workshop to think about the next year's products, you just have to stop and say, "Wow! Really?"

Even the size of the room can make a difference. One maxim that Guy uses is, "The bigger the room, the bigger the thinking." He's noticed that when he has teams break out into two separate groups, the group that stays in the large main hall is able to go further faster than the group that gets shuffled into a smaller, breakout room. So one room is half-empty and the other is completely full. The half-empty room invariably does a better job. That dichotomy shows how something as simple as physical surroundings, which are often overlooked, can have a big impact on outcomes.

> Ask yourself how you can put the team in the very best environment to flourish and do creative work.

The Knower leader may try to find the smallest, cheapest meeting room available for offsite meetings and make it work. He might think he just needs chairs and a table, without recognizing what a huge impact that sparseness will have on everyone in the room. Add up the salaries of everyone there, and it becomes obvious that he could really be sabotaging himself by skimping. It's the Learners who are willing to invest because they know they're going to get it back at the end of the journey.

Remember Mr. Cho's call for respect? His focus is all about a fundamental respect for others. If you give people a great environment in which to work, you're showing that you respect and value them. Give them food and a nice setting when you've got a big challenge ahead of you, and you'll help them feel respected right off the bat.

The Scope

The next thing to be mindful of is what we call scope. What is scope? Scope is a derivative of a clear problem statement, an explicit delineation of the topics surrounding a problem that are "in scope," meaning appropriate to discuss in the meeting. Equally important are those items that are "out of scope," or not appropriate for the discussion because the team doesn't have the authority, permission, or expertise to consider these items at this time.

> Ask yourself what's in scope and appropriate for this conversation, and what's out of scope.

For example, if the conversation is about work schedules, you might say that the focus of this meeting is on normal work hours and that overtime policies, flextime, and vacation are to be discussed at another time. You want to be very clear and explicit about such limitations from the outset.

You want to be clear about the scope for your own purposes and also to get agreement from the team. It can help to draw a map that shows what's in scope and what's out so everyone can visualize what the sandbox looks like, because if you don't delineate the sandbox correctly, then the conversation can wander off and go nowhere.

The Zoom

Another thing we can actively manage is what we call the zoom of the conversation. The zoom means the level of detail that's important for the kind of problem you're solving. Understanding the appropriate level of zoom is critical;

then, through questions and guidance, you can make sure the team is working at the right level. You don't want people to wander off into giant existential questions. On the other hand, sometimes people are so eager to share the details of what they do that it makes it hard to get the conversation moving toward something that yields a real positive change.

What can also happen is that people will brainstorm great ideas for trying an experiment, and someone will say, "Yeah, but how are we going to do X?" and it's really a fine detail. If you spend your time considering reasons why something won't work, especially small ones, you'll never try the experiment. So pulling people back zoom-wise to get the group to what we call the "right flight level" allows great conversations to happen without getting bogged down in fine details.

GUY ON MANAGING WHAT'S HAPPENING ON YOUR STAGE

When a leader actively manages what's happening on his stage, all the elements are and should be fair game to get to the desired outcome. I was fortunate to work with a Dale Carnegie master trainer who brought a team of people to visit my factory. After a productive morning, we headed off for lunch, and among the guests was Jim Wolmack, a renowned author in the world of continuous improvement.

When we got to the restaurant, something occurred that happens all the time. We all stood around, looking at each other, trying to decide who should sit where. Some people didn't want to be so presumptuous as to sit next to the famous author. Others were eager to. You could just see the tension. The Dale Carnegie instructor named Bill Carman pointed decisively at individuals and told them where to sit.

After the meeting, I told him that, at first glance, I thought it was a little rude for him to do what he did. He said, "It's my responsibility during this gathering to ensure that we reach a goal we all want, and that means having the right people sit near one other so they can have the conversations they need to have for us to get where we want to go." Managing the setting and the seating helps you achieve your goal.

Interestingly enough, most people who organize social gatherings understand the importance of the seating chart to pull off a successful event. You really do need to actively manage these kinds of details because what's said and who sits where can affect the tone that is set. It's all part of the idea that we are the owners of the stage. As the leaders, we are the directors of the event. The director needs to worry about all the details, large and small, to make sure that the event unfolds seamlessly. That dedication does not mean ordering people around or being rude, but, when in doubt, you own the stage and it's your job, as leader, to put the right things in the right place.

CHAPTER 7

Engaging Knowers and Learners in Continuously Productive Conversations

We've talked a lot about how you, as a leader, can prepare yourself to approach situations from a Learner mindset, and how you can set the stage for the best possible outcome. But once you're prepared, how do you maintain the momentum? How do you monitor the progress of a meeting or conversation and optimize the open spirit and creativity that will lead you to your desired outcome? How do you effectively steer people back when they get off track? This chapter is about the skills and techniques you need to lead productive conversations from beginning to end. That starts with an ability to read the energy in the room: the mood, tone, and general conditions that prevail.

READING THE ENERGY IN A ROOM

It's important that the Learner leader be able to read the energy of a room. Every meeting or exchange has a kind of arc, and that arc has a starting place. Often it starts with people coming in with curiosity, and then it builds from there around interest. As the meeting goes on, there's a point where the arc can plateau. Ultimately, that arc starts to drop, and that shifting energy is something the Learner leader, who has the skill to observe, can manage. We've all been in meetings where the arc has started to dive, and the meeting participants feel it. Everyone becomes twitchy and starts pulling out cell phones. They're multitasking, and yet the person up front keeps pushing. From our perspective, that's more of a Knower environment, and not an environment where you'll find robust innovation and creativity.

Whenever you walk into an exchange or meeting, start off by noticing the energy, because if you notice it, you can do something about it. You can get people reengaged when the energy starts to lag, sometimes even by throwing out a simple question such as, "What's going on right now? How can we make a difference? Are we making a difference?"

Ask yourself how well you read
a room when it's your meeting.
What are three things you can
do to shift the energy if the arc
is flat-lining?

To read a room, you have to get out of your own head so you can look out and say, "What have I got here?" We have both developed the skill of walking into a room and immediately reading the emotion there. Is the room safe? Are people curious? Are they happy? Are they sad? There's an empathic way that some leaders have of getting a sense of what's occurring. We let that inform us as to what we need to do to get the right conditions in the room.

Not everyone has developed this skill of observation, but there are always things you can do to get a sense of what's happening. Start with eye contact, literally observing how people are looking at you, how eager they are for dialogue and exchange. You can ask teams to close all laptops so you can get a better sense of this.

It's also useful to start meetings with an exercise that gets everybody participating in some sort of relatively safe and benign activity. A lot of people use icebreakers and other facilitation techniques, but the general idea is to give everyone a reason to speak so you can listen and understand the mood and style of the individuals. You'll notice who is willing to participate or who sits with arms folded, looking with some caution at you as if to say, "Why are we here?"

EXERCISE FOR STARTING A MEETING

A powerful exercise to start meetings and get everyone actively participating is to write the following sentence on a flip chart and then ask participants to finish it: "This will have been a great use of our time if..."

Whoever has an idea comes up and writes on a sticky note what their hope or aspiration is for the engagement and posts it on the wall. The things people write will give you a sense of whether they're angry and frustrated or open to really thinking big. Sometimes, people even think they're in a meeting for a completely wrong purpose, and you can redirect them right away by using this approach.

This gives you an opportunity to understand where people are before you launch into the real content of any meeting. Imagine looking at a race car sitting in the pit, and you have no idea if that car can perform. The only way you can tell is if it's in motion. What you really want to do is get people in motion and working as opposed to launching right into an intense dialogue in which four-fifths of the group don't have a chance to speak for the first half hour. Get everybody involved so you can sense who is genuinely engaged and who is not.

ALLAN ON THE POWER OF CALLING OUT
WHAT IS NOT BEING SAID

I was facilitating a meeting for a Fortune 200 company, during which a very heated conversation boiled up. Some team members were feeling uncomfortable, some became silent, and some looked withdrawn. It was tough for a while, and then the energy plummeted. I'd worked with this group before and they were familiar with my use of the term *energy* in a room, so I stopped and said, "What's the energy in this room? What's going on? What needs to be said?" I got everyone's attention because I was calling out what was happening.

Finally, one of the senior leaders said, "Well, I think we've been in some heavy, intense conversation and maybe we're done for the day." I waited for another senior leader to make a statement from a different perspective, but no one said anything, so I honored that and we finished the meeting. As I was wrapping up, another senior leader came over to me and said, "Wow, I thought you did a great job of getting us to look at some things today. I didn't think we were done at all. In fact, I thought we were just getting to the meat of the situation when my colleague suggested we stop." I paused before replying, "What might have happened had you voiced this opinion during the meeting?" Sometimes, the most beneficial thing you can do in a meeting is to stop moving through the agenda and, instead, check on how the meeting is actually going.

MONITORING YOUR REACTIONS

Part of reading the energy of a room is watching what effect your reactions are having on people. It's important to recognize that leaders can shut down creativity and innovative thinking without knowing they're doing it. In other words, you could have the right room and the right participants wanting to engage, but if you fall into a Knower mindset and respond with a high degree of control, you may shoot down ideas and cap innovative thinking.

This misdirection often happens when leaders get angry or frustrated because they're not getting the responses they want or because they're confronted with a Knower mindset that's not easy to change. It's important not to respond to those kinds of situations by lapsing into your own Knower mindset. Regression will actually kill the dialogue and keep people from being able to reach the goals you've set. Looking back to Chapter 1, where we identified where we fell on the Knower-Leader spectrum, we want to recognize 1) where our set point is, and 2) what sort of situations trigger us to move in one direction or another. It's important to keep track of our own energy and mindset while we're watching out for others and reading their energy.

WATCHING YOUR LANGUAGE

The language you choose when you walk into a room goes a long way toward getting people to engage and recognize that they have permission to think in a more expansive way than, perhaps, they have in the past. One of the techniques Guy uses with groups is to banish the word *pilot* from discussions about trying something new and, instead, use the word *experiment*. This may not sound like a big distinction, but if you run an experiment, you can get everybody to agree on what you're hoping to learn, and every experiment is successful because we learn from it. When people join in a pilot, and that pilot doesn't go the way it's been designed to go, those people have just spent their chips on a failed pilot.

Guy likes to use the phrase *small simple reversible experiments*, or SSREs, instead of the term *pilots*. You can ask the group, "What would happen if we did a small experiment here?" or "What kind of experiment would prove your idea?" People are eager to participate in small experiments, particularly if they're reversible. It takes the pressure off when they realize this isn't a permanent policy that shakes the foundation of the business, but something simple to try. If it's successful, they can use it going forward. If it's not, they've still learned something. Getting people into that mindset and letting them know it's okay to try things is a very effective way to engage people and open their minds.

OPEN-SPIRITED LANGUAGE

To kick off conversations in an open-spirited way, you can use any of the following sentence openers to get respondents thinking out loud:

"What would have to be true for . . . to happen?"

"What would happen if . . . ?"

"I wonder . . . ?"

"Have we considered . . . ?"

"What would be a great use of our time if we . . . ?"

KEY STEPS FOR LEADING PRODUCTIVE CONVERSATIONS

You want the room to have an open energy, but how do you make that happen? We've broken it down into five steps that you can follow from a meeting's opening to its end.

Step 1: Find some way, early in the meeting, to engage people. It may be only two or three people or it may be a large group, but, either way, make sure you get everybody participating and use open-spirited language to get started. The first step is simply to get a conversation flowing, because from there, you can start to read the room. Unless people speak, it's very hard to tell what's going on between their ears. You've got to get people active in order to help guide the group to creative thinking.

Step 2: Get the group to talk through their assumptions. What are all of the different things that they believe as they come into this situation? These are things that they believe to be true or historical precedents that are preventing them from broader thinking. Then, start to challenge those assumptions. Pick one and say, "Let's go ahead and discuss this topic, but let's assume it's not true anymore." Guy told the story in Chapter 4 about the pathology lab where no one thought it was possible to turn around test results more quickly until the scientists started challenging some assumptions about how they worked. That opened up the dialogue, and allowed ideas to flow more freely. Get the assumptions out on the table, and then actively try to break down one or two to show that you're serious about stretching people's thinking.

Step 3: The third step is to ask the group, "What kinds of things could knock us off track? How might we be completely surprised, either by competitors or a technology that might come and knock us sideways?" Again, aim to get people talking about things that are almost unimaginable. You do this not because you expect to get perfect answers, but rather because you want to stimulate people's minds in open-spirited discussions.

Step 4: Brainstorm with the group in more than one way to move ideas forward to meet your goals. Maybe even break a few rules, but still focus on things you all think you could achieve. Be forward looking and ask, "What kind of experiment could we run to learn more?"

Step 5: The final piece is to be sure to close the conversation with a careful discussion about the what, the who, and the when. You should ask, "What are we going to do, by when, and who's going to be the owner of this?" We need to set up clear expectations for the completion of the plans. Let people know that you expect results as well as great creative ideas. You do that by closing the conversation with a clear sense of accountability. We call this action planning.

If you do this step right, the next time you get together you can say, "How are we doing? Where do we stand?" This is really important because we've seen really powerful brainstorming sessions with teams whose members then walk out of the room and let their daily responsibilities get in the way. All of a sudden, they're not making progress, even though they had a very meaningful discussion. Frankly, such a meeting is completely wasteful.

LEARNING TO LISTEN

You can't be a good leader in a conversation, and you can't ask effective questions that challenge assumptions unless you have the skills to really listen. Such listening incorporates an understanding, not just of what people are saying, but also what their tone and body language are projecting. Understanding and applying these clues allows you to lead truly productive conversations.

The coaching industry requires that professional coaches develop a heightened level of listening. Allan became certified in the 1990s at CTI (The Coaches Training Institute). It is one of the top schools in the world; tens of thousands of professional certified coaches have passed through its doors. The leaders teach a very simple, very powerful, listening model called Listening 1, 2, 3, which really helps students understand the context of listening by imagining that it has three levels.

The following has been taken from the book, *Co-Active Coaching*, written by Henry and Karen Kimsey House, and Laura Whitworth, in which they describe the three levels of listening:

Level I: Internal Listening

At Level I, our attention is on *ourselves*. We listen to the words of the other person, but our focus is on what it means to us. At Level I, the spotlight is on me: my thoughts, my judgments, my feelings, and my conclusions about myself and others. Whatever is happening with the other person is coming back to me through a diode: a one-way energy trap that lets information in but not out. I'm absorbing information by listening but holding it in a trap that recycles it. At Level I, there is only one question; what does this mean to me? There are many times when this is entirely appropriate; for instance, when you are traveling alone to a different city, you are likely to be operating at Level I most of the time. It may be perfectly reasonable that all of your attention is on yourself.

Level II: Focused Listening

At Level II, there is a sharp focus on the *other person*. You can see it in people's posture when they are communicating at Level II: probably both leaning forward and looking intently at each other. A great deal of attention is focused on the other person and there is not much awareness of the outside world.

Level III: Global Listening

At Level III, you listen at 360 degrees. In fact, you listen as though you and the other person are aware of everything around you as you speak. Here you have the ability to observe yourself, the other person, and the space around you. You let all three elements inform your intuition. Level III includes everything you can observe with your senses: what you see, hear, smell, and feel—the tactile sensations as well as the emotions that are playing out. Level III includes the action, the inaction, and the interaction.

Listening is a skill that can be practiced and developed. You can help yourself along the path of self-management by recognizing when you're going internal (level one), and then getting back to level two. Then, as you achieve mastery around that level, you can start to integrate the clues in the room. When you're listening at level three, you will pick up information that you can use to direct people toward new thinking and move the conversation to a new level.

To really engage people in productive conversations, you first want to get them talking by asking them open-spirited questions. Then, you want to listen not only to what they say but to how they say it, picking up on all the details of tone, body language, and other external things that will help you gauge whether they're ready to stretch their thinking and move forward. It's really a combination of participating in the interaction and simultaneously being able to look at it from the outside and recognize that this is a group process which you are hosting. We'll talk further about your role as host in the next chapter.

ALLAN ON READING YOUR AUDIENCE

Years ago, I was asked to facilitate a change management workshop for a national railroad company where layoffs were being announced for the first time in the iconic transportation company's history. When I walked into the room, I was staring at 100 men in their 50s and 60s, most of whom were celebrating 30 and 40 years of seniority. As I scanned the room, face after face told me they were angry, scared, and disinterested in this mandatory meeting with a facilitator half their age speaking to them about the positive elements of change.

My desired outcome was for them to explore options and think outside the box about what their futures could hold. As I set up my laptop, I realized the environment wasn't right for the presentation I'd prepared. They were in no mood for a creativity session to explore possibilities, but I was being paid to do a job and couldn't leave. What to do? I took a deep breath, closed my laptop, and said, "Gentlemen, this sucks." I was a bit horrified those words came out of my mouth, but it was all I could think to say. To my surprise, laughter emerged from the group, so I asked, "What if we could talk about what might be positive about your current situation?" After that, many members of the group began to speak about the big payoffs and pensions with which they were being gifted, and others spoke about how they were nearing retirement and how extra payout allowed many options. A couple of outliers remained, but overall, the conversation shifted from fear and despair to fruitful exchanges about a path forward.

If I hadn't been able to use my level-three listening to read and work with the energy in the room, I might not have left that room upright. But, working with what the room was asking for, even if it meant going off script, allowed for major learning to happen.

CHAPTER 8

Accessing Your Optimal Operating State

his chapter is about understanding your operating state and how to access an optimal state, particularly when you get thrown off your game because of triggers, limiting beliefs, or simply a foul mood that overtakes you. Learner leaders understand how to achieve a place of calm and flow in their daily responsibilities. They know when they're in their optimal operating state and when they're not. They take time to reflect on what conditions allow them to be in an optimal state as opposed to a weakened or depleted state. You can do this by instituting regular mood checks throughout your day and asking yourself, "How is my operating state?

Am I feeling empowered, strong, and confident, or am I in a bad mood, not feeling on top of my game?"

We all get thrown out of our optimal operating state from time to time. We land in a vulnerable state where our sea legs are a little wobbly and we're not standing on solid ground. When this happens, the important thing is to recognize the condition and know what to do to get back into our optimal operating states.

WHAT TO WATCH OUT FOR

In Chapter 6, we addressed the carefully planned steps for a powerful engagement, but what are some of the things to watch out for, hazards along the way that can jeopardize a smooth engagement? When you get thrown off your game, there are two categories of pitfalls that are likely to interfere with powerful leading.

There are internal pitfalls, or things that come from your own mood or beliefs, and external pitfalls, or problems that arise because of the environment, conditions, or team dynamics.

Internal Pitfalls:

⇨ You are triggered and you lose control.

⇨ You are triggered and don't recognize you're increasing your chances of moving to a Knower mindset.

⇨ The trigger(s) produce limiting beliefs that throw you off your game.

⇨ Your mind enters the F.U.D. zone (fear, uncertainty, and/or doubt).

⇨ You create a sense of "urgency" when it is not required.

⇨ You create a false sense of urgency that you have to push through regardless of perceived difficulty.

⇨ You zoom in, or have tunnel vision, so you're focused on details, prescriptions, and directives instead of the big picture.

External Pitfalls:

⇨ The environmental conditions are bad for conversation.

⇨ Other individual(s) are not in shape for the conversation; they may be triggered, coming from a Knower mindset, or trapped by limiting beliefs.

⇨ Decisions are being made from a vulnerable operating state.

⇨ You may fail to recognize the historical precedents.

⇨ You do not have the authority or permission to make changes you and your team identify.

These are all circumstances that weaken leadership and put us on an unproductive path. Our ability to identify this misdirection is attributable to the brain research we discussed in previous chapters. When you are triggered, when something catches you off guard and starts to generate fear, uncertainty, or doubt, when you are not careful, your automatic brain, the part that tells you to fight or run, will take control. In this framework of asking genuine, creative questions, it's important not to let yourself slide down that slope.

We need to avoid reactions that are based solely on patterns, which is what the lizard brain will do. It will say, "Uh oh, I've seen this before. I'd better take action." Imagine that you went to the doctor, and as soon as you walked in, the doctor said, "Nice to meet you. Here's your prescription for cholesterol and blood pressure medications." You would probably say, "Wait a second. You haven't tested my blood or checked my blood pressure yet." To which he'd reply, "Yes, but you're 45 years old, you're not as thin as you used to be, and the last three people who were in here needed those prescriptions, so I'm going to give them to you, too."

You'd be shocked, wouldn't you? Yet, that's what happens when you rely on automatic, pattern-based responses to situations. If we don't spend a little time zeroing in and getting real facts and information, the only thing we can do is give a response based on old patterns. In his book, *Thinking Fast and Slow* (mentioned earlier), Daniel Kahneman describes how "thinking fast activity," the stuff that happens in your automatic brain, is relatively effortless. It takes extra active energy to think, plan, and work your way through difficult situations. The key challenge is to think slowly.

We suggest you do this by pulling yourself back, zooming your perspective out a little to look at the whole scene, and then saying, "I can manage this, I have control, and I'm driving this situation." Think about how athletes on ski slopes literally envision each of their moves before they compete. The same can be true for the leader. If the leader can recognize the negative voices or thoughts in his head and grab hold of those thoughts, he can then manage them and try to see things from a different perspective. Remember, you're not just an actor on a stage reacting to what is happening; you are the director. You can redirect the situation and create a clear, positive path forward.

GUY ON THE POWER OF SLOWING THINGS DOWN

I was working with a team of cardiologists at a major medical center on a group effort to redesign the way appointments were made and how patients were brought into the facility. We had gathered all the doctors and the support staff who handled scheduling from a nearby call center.

We got approximately 30 people together in a room, had them slow down and get away from the stresses of their day-to-day activities, and told them to leave their business cards outside the door so that everyone was equally authorized to speak. About halfway through our first morning, one of the cardiac surgeons said, "Wait a minute. We have to stop for a minute. I just have to do something here." He walked over to a young lady who was one of the schedulers, reached out his hand and said, "You know, you've been scheduling and managing my life for five years, and I've never met you. I'm embarrassed, and I'm sorry. It's really important that we understand how each other's work goes so that we can both get the most out of this and create a great opportunity for patients."

You could have heard a pin drop in the room because cardiac surgeons are not necessarily known for leading with thoughtfulness and care. That story really shook the ground and caused everybody to realize that every person has something to offer if given the chance.

When you slow down the process and make a close, personal connection with those around you, it makes all the difference to the team dynamic, resulting in increased collaboration, contribution, and engagement.

BIG CHALLENGES, AND WHAT YOU CAN DO ABOUT THEM

Many times in our fast-paced work environments, we're thrown off our game and triggered externally by something we don't agree with, or triggered internally by limiting beliefs or thoughts that evoke fear and doubt. When such upsets occur, we move out of the ideal conditions for leading with a Learner mindset and we default to the Knower mindset to survive the conversation. An example of this happened in the 2014 Winter Olympics, when the US speed skating team was expected to bring home a significant cache of medals. Just before the games, their sponsor delivered new high-tech suits which were supposed to offer a competitive advantage. When the first event went poorly, the team questioned whether the new suits had led to the loss. This small doubt bloomed in the athletes' heads, contributing to no medals in that sport for the US team, regardless of what uniforms they wore.

We all, at times, produce limiting beliefs that hold us back. Limiting beliefs are thoughts we conjure up in our minds that are linked to fear, doubt, or anxiety and cause us to hit the brakes on creative, innovative new thinking (usually due to fear of failing). The irony of limiting beliefs is that there is no physical evidence to justify them, but they feel very true and real. Limiting beliefs can start small and grow to the point where you're paralyzed by them and do not pursue what you truly want to pursue. They can be false impressions we can create (e.g., I will not be successful) or that develop subtly in our roles as adults, personally or professionally.

"If I let go of control, I'll fail." "If I delegate this, it won't get done the right way." "I won't be seen as successful if I don't get this project perfect." These are examples of limiting beliefs we often see in executives. Thoughts like these can be wired firmly into people's thinking, keeping them in a prison cell of inaction or inappropriate action. They are just an illusion, because they stem from thinking that is not needed anymore.

> Ask yourself how often you notice when you've been triggered. How frequently do you recognize when a limiting belief has emerged in your mind, along with a feeling of anxiety, fear, or doubt? What impact does your triggered state have on your leadership? How can you increase your ability to notice when you get triggered so you can get back to a Learner mindset?

What's important is to pause for a moment and reflect on limiting beliefs you may be playing out right now which are related to something on which you are working. Write down the limiting beliefs and notice how they may be connected to fear, doubt, or anxiety. Examine them to see if there is any evidence (physical or tangible) to validate them.

NOT NOTICING

The most common and most major pitfall is when you're not noticing your own impact, your mood, or the quality of your operating state. If you're clueless, you're really dead in the water without any hope of change happening.

The quality of our leadership is tied directly to our ability to be self-aware. A high level of self-management is required to recognize both what we know and what we do not know, but that's the beauty of Learners. Learners will invest the time and effort. They are always interested in developing new skills and curious about their impact and how to take it to the next level.

Becoming a master of self-awareness and self-management starts with making a habit of checking on your mental state. If need be, set an alarm to remind yourself to do this regularly, and ask yourself:

➪ What's my mood when I wake up in the morning?

➪ What's my mood when I arrive at work?

➪ What's my mood at lunch?

➪ What's my mood before going into a meeting or a one-on-one exchange?

⇨ What's my mood when I arrive home?

These mood management checks will help you become aware, but they are only the first steps. They'll help you decide whether you're in an optimal operating state or a vulnerable one. If you find you're in a vulnerable operating state, you can help yourself through it by doing the following:

⇨ Scan for limiting beliefs. Limiting beliefs are imaginary, but they bring a dark cloud into a leader's mind that casts a shadow of doubt and fear. An example might be: "It is the first day of the month and we won't achieve our target revenues this month."

⇨ Check to see if there is any truth (specific, physical, evidence) in the limiting belief. In the example above, there is not any truth because it is a future statement; you will have a whole month to create the results!

⇨ Consider flipping the limiting belief to a powerful assumption. A powerful assumption is also made up, but it moves the leader out of a place of fear and doubt into one of hope and possibility. An example might be this: "With the brainpower we have and a renewed focus, we are in excellent shape to meet our revenue targets."

⇨ Let your level-three listening inform you of where you should focus your attention to foster the best conditions for a meeting or conversation.

EXAMPLES OF LIMITING BELIEFS (LB) AND POWERFUL ASSUMPTIONS (PA)

LB: I can't let go of control or the results will be poor.

PA: By delegating effectively, I'm allowing my team to stretch and build their skills, and I'm able to focus on higher-value work.

LB: I have to take the lead in senior meetings to ensure I look good.

PA: If I allow my team to excel and place the spotlight on them, showcasing their results, the value of my own leadership brand will increase.

LB: If I say, "I don't know" to a colleague, I will appear weak and ineffective.

PA: Having the strength to say, "I don't know. Let's look at this together," allows my colleagues to see my humanity and allows us to solve the issue together, increasing collaboration and knowledge.

ALLAN ON THE POSITIVE AND NEGATIVE VOICES IN OUR HEADS

In the 1990s, I worked at a career management consulting firm which was a cosponsor of the Atlanta Olympics, and I had the opportunity after the games to provide career consulting to a few Olympians who were asking the question, "What do I do with the rest of my life?" I was very curious to learn how these young adults managed not to lose their competitive potential when faced with the pressure of a global audience. I remember saying to the first one I met, "I get how you became so good at your sport, but how did you manage to not freak out when millions of people were watching you and you were representing the entire United States of America? How were you able to hold it together?"

I asked that question of several athletes, and I was struck by the fact that they all, basically, said the same thing: There was always a voice in their heads telling them they might fail, but then there was this other voice that was very empowering and had a mood of hope and possibility. They just chose to listen to the second voice and remind themselves that they were well prepared and totally qualified to be there.

Those athletes had the ability to hear two different voices, manage the internal conversation, and then make a choice. And they chose to listen to their inner champion. In my book *Bold Moves*, we used that idea metaphorically. We included a fable in which we called that negative voice the inner critic and the positive voice, the Whisperer. We named the positive voice the Whisperer because, a lot of times, the negative voice distracts us severely with external noise. If we have a quarter-million-dollar sound system lodged in our head, we will never hear that quiet flash of intuition. What was really interesting about these Olympians was that they had the ability to self-manage and get the noise volume down so they could listen to the more compelling champion, or Whisperer, voice, which said, "You're good to go."

I thought that such an ability was extraordinarily impressive, particularly since most of the athletes were barely 20 years old. I was so struck by this learning that I integrated it into my leadership coaching. Over the years in my coaching business, a significant number of leaders have truly embraced this concept; it has proved to be a game changer in their personal leadership.

FALSE URGENCY

In Chapter 2, we spoke about urgency. Many can recall a time growing up when people went to the mailbox once a day. Now, millions of us check our e-mail dozens of times throughout the day. In our over stimulated world, a lot of people exist in a sort of head-down, plow-through, adrenaline-rush state. Allan and Guy refer to this condition as "false urgency." That phrase pertains to when people get into a vulnerable operating state, when they feel the need to control, or when they accelerate the situation just to move through it, even though they're not in the best state to do so. Of course, you can imagine the consequences.

Because of the speed at which things happen today and the high potential for distraction, it's really important that you self-manage and develop some discipline so you're not wasting your energy. You have to discipline yourself to keep your focus where it needs to be. Recognize and preserve your optimal operating state to accomplish your best work throughout the course of the day. Instead of ramping up and going to *urgent*, which may be your natural instinct, you can choose to slow down and go to *pause*. Slowing down allows you to notice your mindset and realize that your operating state may not be ideal. With that realization, you can recalibrate. When you can recalibrate, the false urgency dissipates and Learner leadership elevates.

In work environments where constant interruptions are the norm, the easy path to take is jumping to an automatic, quick response. Avoiding that reaction requires practice and skill; it is not necessarily something that will come naturally. You are going to have to really push yourself to slow down, and practice it to get great results. We are not suggesting that you should go slowly; we just ask that you start off slowly and thoughtfully, so the rest of what you do can be fast and smooth, producing better results.

> Ask yourself how often you create a sense of urgency about things that don't need attention immediately? How can you slow down so you stop creating false urgency for yourself and others? Pause, and ask yourself, "Is what I am asking for really needed *now?*"

NOT HAVING ALL THE ANSWERS

What happens when you don't have the all answers and that apparent lack of knowledge makes you nervous? This topic is a great one to look at through the lens of how the Knower leader operates versus the Learner leader operates. Both will handle the situation in profoundly different ways. If you think back to the chart in the first chapter, Knowers are about control, saving face, and looking good. They may have a reduced level of self-esteem or an unhealthy ego, which is probably why they feel they have to know all the answers.

One of the great attributes of many top leaders today is an ability to say, "You know, I don't know, but we'll figure it out together," or, "I don't know, but I'll find out and get back to you." What's so powerful about this response is it displays the humanity of those leaders. They are prepared to show vulnerability; they acknowledge that they can't possibly know everything. Having the guts to admit such self-awareness is actually going to score you higher points as a leader than if you were to pretend to know something you don't.

Saying you "don't know" can also create a shared future. The whole team becomes jointly accountable for results as you attempt to find answers together. In the old mindset, the Knower would prepare in advance and then walk into a meeting and tell everybody exactly what has to happen and why. That old mindset can produce a lot of unnecessary pressure. In the new mindset, the Learner can do some homework to find out what he doesn't know and then bring questions to the team. The pitfall is when you are triggered by the circumstance, and it causes nervousness or fear. The opportunity you have, as a Learner, is to embrace the challenge and bring it to your team in a spirit of, "I don't know, we don't know, but we can figure it out and we have the very best people in the room to do it. So let's go."

DEFENSIVENESS

What happens when you or someone else becomes defensive? We all know how easily defensiveness can insert itself into a conversation when someone is feeling angry or shocked or experiences some other negative emotion. Defensiveness may result in one of the fastest slides imaginable into a Knower mindset. When people become defensive, they tend to activate fully all the characteristics of the Knower mindset.

There are two sides to this coin. Tails is when you yourself become defensive. When you succumb to the temptation, you really have to manage your mood. If you find yourself feeling defensive, you have to do the same thing we've spoken about before, which is to pause and figure out what the triggering event was. Once you understand what happened, then you can ask yourself, "What can I do to minimize this feeling and take the heat off this moment so I can return to my optimal operating state?"

Sometimes, depending on what the issue is and your level of mastery, you have the ability to diffuse your defensive feelings in the moment and restore your Learner mindset in real time. In other circumstances, you might have to stop and take a break. You could say, "Look, we have to pick this up later." If you're so thrown off that your operating state cannot be optimal in the moment, then taking a break is what you need to do.

As you spend additional time in the Learner mindset, you'll develop the ability to simply "call it." That means stopping to explain the defensive feelings. You'll often find that those who caused your defensiveness didn't intend that reaction, so give them a chance to clear up what they meant. As you can imagine, when we're triggered, too often we don't do the extra work of verifying what really happened. We swallow the feeling or move into behavior that stems from the Knower mindset, which weakens the quality of the conversation and the results of that conversation.

The other side of the coin is when you're in an exchange and you notice someone else has been triggered. We spoke previously about the responsibility of the leader to notice when something is off. You might notice that the person you are talking to is flushed, her jaw has tightened, or her eye contact has shifted. Her tone might also have changed. Her words might sound all right, but the context around the words will inform you if something is disquieting. When you perceive such circumstances, you can freeze the actual conversation to check on its process. You might say, "Let me just stop for a second and check in. How are you doing? Is something I said throwing you off? What's going on?"

The person you're talking to might reply with something such as, "When you said that, I felt very intimidated, as if I'm not doing my job," even if that was not what you intended. In such likely cases, your intention can be verified very quickly as long as you pause and check in. When you restore an optimal operating state and continue the conversation from a Learner perspective, we suggest that you accelerate to your goals quickly.

The thing to keep in mind with defensiveness, as with all triggers, is that not handling these moments can cause big rifts. It can cause a permanent relationship breakdown. So often, it's all just over a misunderstanding. The simple act of noticing, checking in, and resolving these issues when they happen can have an amazing effect. You diffuse situations before they escalate and get all the parties aligned to move forward to an optimal place.

CONTENT VERSUS PROCESS

The following scenarios will give you a sense of the different ways people are affected by the content of what you say versus the process, which is the body language, tone, and behaviors wrapped around the words that are spoken.

- A team member has just given a presentation that you think could have been more thorough. After he's done, you say, in front of five or six other people in the conference room, "I think you could do x, y, and z a bit better next time." This leaves him feeling embarrassed, angry, defensive, and in no mood to take your suggestion to heart. Instead, imagine if you had a side conversation stating, "You gave a good presentation and your thinking made me curious; if we could explore x, y, and z, what might be possible?" This conversation could produce a very positive, solid, empowering outcome.

- You have just completed a meeting that didn't go well and are running to another. You don't notice that you're still frustrated and not in your optimal operating state as you find your seat at the head of the next crowded table. As you begin to speak, you see the handouts you requested aren't done to your satisfaction and you frown at your assistant. Your assistant's face turns red, which you don't notice, but the team does. Ten minutes into the meeting, you feel the room is stuffy and people are offering nothing but yes and no responses. You click back into your optimal operating state and realize you arrived triggered from your prior meeting. You stop mid-sentence and say, "Team, I need to apologize. When I arrived, I was frustrated from a prior meeting. I did not mean to bring that negativity into this meeting." Then you look at your assistant and say, "I'm sorry about the look. I know I didn't circle back with you regarding the handout, and that's my error, not yours." You move back to the agenda and, within minutes, the room feels different. The conversation is richer and more robust and team members are leaning in, not out. By recognizing the impact your mood had and stopping the meeting to clean up the mess, you allowed the team to self-correct, resulting in increased trust, collaboration, and interest.

CLOSE-MINDEDNESS

What happens when you sense that a person or an entire team has become close-minded? Maybe their answers to your open, friendly questions have shut down the conversation and let you know they're in no mood for thoughtful activities. They're posturing, maybe even in an adversarial way.

This really falls into the realm of negotiations, and there are whole bodies of work on this subject, such as Bill Ury's *Getting to Yes*. When someone is being adversarial or close-minded, one of the best-known techniques is to force yourself to slow down and explore any or all of the things that you *can* agree on. Maybe it's something as basic as, "Well, at least we can agree that we have to finish this with a contract," or "We can agree that by the time we walk out of here, x, y, and z needs to be true, because otherwise it's a waste of our time."

The key idea is to reach across the table and try to get joint agreement on something when you sense resistance; start getting people to say yes, which is really a kind of possibility thinking. That's why Ury's book is titled *Getting to Yes*. The idea is that we have to identify areas where we can agree so we can create some kind of bond before we move forward.

THE ADVANTAGE OF OBSERVING YOU

The quality of your leadership is in direct proportion to your ability to self-manage by knowing how to monitor your own operating state. Learner leadership allows you to know when you are in your optimal operating state—and when you have slipped out of it—as well as how to get back to that desired place when you slip. Most important is your ability to notice because, unless you are curious enough to check in with yourself on a regular basis throughout the day, you won't have the ability to lead optimally in a consistent way for yourself as an individual, for your colleagues, and for your loved ones.

CHAPTER 9

Prepare to Engage

Albert Einstein once advised, "Never memorize something you can look up." In this chapter, we offer a structured framework for thinking about categories of questions you may want to ask. We also provide a table with three time frames: Yesterday, Today and Tomorrow, set against three different domains: Purpose, Process and People. We call this structure the Completeness Framework and believe that it is an easy way to make sure you have not forgotten an entire category of inquiry. For example, in solving a problem, you may want to ask, "Who in the past has worked on a similar issue?" Using the framework in the following table, this topic would come from the "Yesterday" column and the "People" row. You can use this table of questions to help you and your team gain the expertise needed to solve crucial problems and improve the way you do business.

THE COMPLETENESS FRAMEWORK

The framework we use to explore the completeness of our thinking is simple. The table is designed to help the leader do a quick but thorough check before engaging with colleagues on a problem or opportunity. In any given situation, you may only need to think carefully through two or three of the boxes in the following table, but by running through the table in its entirety, you can build confidence that you have not left out a major topic simply because you're in a rush to resolve a situation.

	Yesterday	Today	Tomorrow
Purpose			
Process			
People			

The table is organized, first, from left to right in columns from "Yesterday," or historical and background information; to "Today," or current facts; and into "Tomorrow," or future visions, ideas, and actions. Next, the table is organized in three rows, from top to bottom: "Purpose," "Process," and "People." These three categories come directly from the writings of James P. Womack, co-author of *Lean Thinking*, the seminal work on how Toyota maintains a learning and continuously improving culture from which most businesses can learn. Jim explains that all businesses, both for-profit and nonprofit, are simply a combination of these three basic elements: purpose, process, and people. Examining the "People" row, for instance, could inspire questions from the "Yesterday," "Today," and "Tomorrow" columns. By using the following framework as a guide, you could be able to quickly scan the boxes and identify or remind yourself of areas you need to fully think through before you engage with a person or your team in resolving a situation. Think of the table as a simple Memory Jogger™ to be sure you haven't forgotten anything prior to engaging.

BRINGING IT ALL HOME

Throughout the book, we have emphasized the importance of pausing and thinking before engaging in a situation. Here, we want to provide a high-level review of the key themes from the book and speak to what you can start applying tomorrow morning.

In this book, we have offered the following roadmap:

1. *Define your purpose (desired outcome):* **When** engaging with another individual or team, decide if the situation requires a structured outcome and define in your mind what your desired outcome might be. Also, understand the scope of the situation (e.g., do you need to engage outside support, sponsors, or individuals to achieve the intended purpose?).

2. *Self-preparedness:* **Ask** what needs attention for you to achieve your purpose. What information do you need to gather to lead the conversation effectively, either in a one-on-one session or a team environment?

3. *Other-preparedness:* Have you provided those involved with the right context, preparatory work, and/or information so that the one-on-one or team engagement can commence in an effective way?

4. *Setting the stage:* Have you set the stage to amplify the potential for creative thinking? This includes timing, the right physical space (onsite/offsite?), and the right players (fresh eyes), so that everyone can engage in a creative and innovative discussion.

5. *Lead from the Learner mindset:* Are you in your optimal operating state, ready to identify and manage any limiting beliefs? Are you willing to challenge existing operating assumptions?

6. *Start small and build your skills:* Leading consistently from the Learner mindset is a skill that you'll need to practice over time to build strength. We're all prone to slipping into a Knower mindset in response to the daily demands placed on us. The goal is to raise your level of self-awareness so that you can calibrate your leadership style toward the Learner mindset. With practice, leaders can shift behaviorally toward this new leadership mindset.

This shift will produce powerful results for themselves, their teams, their customers, their company, their stakeholders, and the company's bottom line.

7. *Practice all of the above with a spirit of respect and humility:* Use authentic questions to push the boundaries of thinking and approach problems with a fundamental belief in the skills and knowledge of the people who do the work.

OUT OF THE QUESTION

We chose the book title, *Out of the Question*, because the phrase is often used by Knowers to shut down a conversation. We hope you can turn the title on its head and see that from *Out of the Question* flow the following benefits:

INDIVIDUAL BENEFITS

Greater self-participation
Purposeful engagement
Less stress (for leader and participants)
Increased loyalty
Enhanced commitment

INCREASED COLLABORATION

Enhanced team engagement
Creative solutions to real challenges
Moving toward high-performance teams
Joint ownership of decisions

WHAT ARE YOU GOING TO DO TOMORROW?

⇨ Put on your self-observer hat and notice your current mood.

   ⇨ Refer to the poker chip exercise (Chapter 3)

   ⇨ Refer to the Knower/Learner quiz (Chapter 1)

⇨ Pause and reflect on your leadership and presence after a meeting or exchange and ask yourself how you performed within the Learner-Knower framework. What worked and what would you do differently next time?

   ⇨ Pause and question.

   ⇨ Adopt a curious mindset.

   ⇨ Listen more than talk.

   ⇨ Actively manage the stage.

   ⇨ Use level two/three listening.

⇨ Use self-reflection and/or solicit feedback by asking a confidant or two to let you know how you are leading in your meetings and exchanges with others.

⇨ Use the list from above to gauge how well you did or are progressing.

⇨ Begin experiments. Look for situations in which you can practice new behaviors with particularly heightened sensitivity toward people. Notice how they respond to these new behaviors.

⇨ Each morning, take time to look at the opportunities in your day to practice Learner skills.

JOIN THE LEARNER LEADER COMMUNITY

Our intention in writing this book was to provide a roadmap for achieving improved results for you and your team by changing the way you behave, lead, and interact with others. Our world is evolving with bewildering rapidity, and today's workforce is much more attuned to, and demanding of, a positive work experience than any previous set of co-workers. The command-and-control days of Henry Ford and the behind-the-lines General are long gone. Today, the most important challenge is to understand how leaders can engage with their teams to tackle jointly the rapidly shifting challenges before them. The Learner leader is ideally suited to make the most of an individual's personal talents and the collective talents of the team.

We want to close with an invitation to join our Learner leader community for a deeper dive than we can produce in this book. We have given you a taste of the kind of detailed thinking that sets the stage for success, but we're well aware that we can only touch on the topic of specialty questions in this format. We would like to invite you to join our web community at **www. TheCuriousLeader.com**, where we host interactive exchanges and provide a place to post and have questions answered or crafted by the community.

Going back to our favorite quote from Louis Pasteur, "Chance favors the prepared mind." We cannot overstate the need to prepare before you engage. Through many years of experience, we have learned that trying to solve problems and make decisions by shooting away with rapid-fire answers based on little preparation is a recipe for poor long-term results and a team that is disengaged. We hope that joining this community will help you prepare yourself for enhanced engagement—and stay on track as you practice the crucial skills of Learner leadership, through which you can engage, inspire, innovate, and win.

About the Authors

ABOUT ALLAN

My work as a professional leadership and performance coach over the past 16 years has centered on using powerful questions. It's at the core of what I believe professional coaching represents. From as early as I can remember, I've been fascinated with human potential and what allows some people to soar in life and others to plateau. Part of that comes from my own experience of growing up in the Midwest, having big questions, and being thrown some curves. I saw how, sometimes, we're not meant to go it alone. I've always been on the psychology side of business, focusing on issues around human potential. I received my undergraduate degree in psychology from Kalamazoo College in Michigan. My undergraduate thesis was on humanistic management. I was selected to work in a paper mill—a very archaic industry back then—and looked at the grievance system used by the mill workers and management, which really meant looking at the human condition.

Early in my career, I worked at Marriott International, where I cycled through a succession of six jobs in sales, marketing, and operations. After that, it became clear I needed to leave the big organization. That resulted in a wake-up call around the age of 30 to become better aligned with what I wanted to do in life. So, I went back to school and earned a master's degree in counseling psychology. I was a bit of rarity in my graduation class as I was clear I did not want to be a psychotherapist. I knew my focus would be on the business world.

During that time, I worked for a global career management company. I consulted in the company's San Francisco office, helping executives who had suddenly found themselves without work. These leaders had great pedigrees and lots of experience, mostly from Fortune 500 or 1000 companies, and many had advanced degrees. It was very powerful to watch these individuals find themselves for the first time in their lives in a place where they didn't know what they were going to do next.

It was through the power of questions that I was able to attain a successful transition rate with my clients, which was recognized within the company. The experience allowed me to lean into professional coaching. One day, back in 1998, I met the founders of one of the top coaching schools on the planet. I enrolled and became a Certified Professional Co-Active Coach, and in 2004 was awarded the Master Certified Coach designation—the highest level of certification by the International Coach Federation. At the time of publishing this book, there were only 620 of us worldwide.

Today, coaching is a $2.4 billion industry annually with a growth rate of about 20 percent a year. There are dozens of niches within professional coaching, but my concentration has been on performance and leadership coaching. I've always been interested in the impact that a coach, one who is solely committed to your desired outcomes, can have. Coaches are not your employer, so they can't fire you, and they're not married to you, so you can't have a divorce. They provide a neutral place and their entire focus is on helping you get to the next level. With hyper change, dwindling resources, and constant demands on organizations to do more with less, coaching has been the perfect avenue to help individuals calibrate their leadership and performance for maximum impact.

This book is really important to me because we are moving too fast in our work worlds today. We are missing opportunities to pause more often in our dialogues with one another and bring a greater sense of curiosity to our exchanges. When we take those opportunities, new thinking emerges and a powerful shift creates increased connection and motivation. This results in a thriving workforce, motivated worker, bold innovation, and success.

ABOUT GUY

My early work experience was as an hourly employee in heavy industry, on production lines. While my friends were at the local swim club, I worked in a welding shop and at a casting and stamping facility. My favorite day of the week was trash day because I could scavenge all sorts of electronics to tear apart and see how they worked. (This was all fine until I tried my skills on our home appliances.) I've always been driven to understand how systems work.

I finished Connecticut College with a job offer in system sales from IBM, but ended up accepting a position with the traditional strategy-consulting house, Bain & Company. At Bain, we spent a significant amount of energy thinking through the personal learning style of our individual clients and the corporate cultures they inhabited. We then crafted presentations to fit their specific needs and styles for maximum impact. Early in my career, I learned that a great idea has little value unless there's a person or team to effectively spread the news.

From there, I took up with a start-up furniture company that Mitt Romney funded through Bain Capital. After a few years, I went to Harvard Business School, where my focus was on production and operations strategy. I quickly learned that a perfect strategy is useless without execution, and that execution boils down to leadership and teamwork.

After Harvard, I met Jim Womack, who is the thought leader in the world of continuous improvement. His specific focus is on the methods of management and learning invented by Toyota, often called lean manufacturing or lean thinking. After working with Jim for several years, I chose to buy my own business, which was a titanium bicycle factory called Merlin. Jim was my partner, advisor, and investor. I ran that company for three years and then sold it and joined with Jim Womack to form the Lean Enterprises Institute, which was a nonprofit institute focused on continuous improvement research. From the Lean Institute, I went out on my own and have spent the past 15 years working as a consultant to help organizations, leaders, and their teams find better ways to get work done and improve their rapport with their customers, colleagues, and suppliers. Most of my process consulting work is wrapped around the overall business system that Toyota uses, which is really about rapid organizational learning and problem-solving. Many people would argue that Toyota's key to success is discovering how to learn better, faster, and more reliably than its competitors.

The inspiration for this book comes from 20-plus years of consulting with firms attempting to make operational and cultural transformations, and from the delight and frustrations of helping teams improve their processes. The spark was really a four-hour plane trip during which I started brainstorming the idea. Allan had been my professional coach for several years, but then our relationship evolved into one in which my process thinking was informing his ideas about performance, and I was integrating his coaching methodology and questioning techniques into my consulting practice. After that plane trip, there was only one person I wanted to call to help me think through my book idea. I called Allan, and the two of us agreed our ideas were a perfect fit.

Contact Allan or Guy directly to
learn more about their services:

Executive Leadership Coaching

Lean Process Consulting

Speaking

Products and Services

Allan Milham	Guy Parsons
BoldMoves Enterprises, Inc.	Value Streams Solutions, LLC.
allan@AllanMilham.com	gparsons@LeanVS.com
480-363-4700	617-484-5454